Daniel Siebert

The Dilemma between Quality Reputation and Risk Prevention

Warranty Provisions of Car Manufacturers

Anchor Academic
Publishing

Siebert, Daniel: The Dilemma between Quality Reputation and Risk Prevention: Warranty Provisions of Car Manufacturers. Hamburg, Anchor Academic Publishing 2014

Buch-ISBN: 978-3-95489-286-0
PDF-eBook-ISBN: 978-3-95489-786-5
Druck/Herstellung: Anchor Academic Publishing, Hamburg, 2014

Bibliografische Information der Deutschen Nationalbibliothek:
Die Deutsche Nationalbibliothek verzeichnet diese Publikation in der Deutschen Nationalbibliografie; detaillierte bibliografische Daten sind im Internet über http://dnb.d-nb.de abrufbar.

Bibliographical Information of the German National Library:
The German National Library lists this publication in the German National Bibliography. Detailed bibliographic data can be found at: http://dnb.d-nb.de

© Anchor Academic Publishing, Imprint der Diplomica Verlag GmbH
Hermannstal 119k, 22119 Hamburg
http://www.diplomica-verlag.de, Hamburg 2014
Printed in Germany

Table of contents

List of Abbreviations

8 D	8 Disciplines, Automotive Quality Method
AAA	American Automobile Association
ACEA	European Automobile Manufacturers Association
AD	Automotive Division
ADAC	Allgemeiner Deutscher Automobilclub e.V.
APAC	Asia Pacific
AVD	Automobilclub von Deutschland
BFH	Bundesfinanzhof, German supreme tax court
BGB	Bürgerliches Gesetzbuch, German code of civil law
BMW	Bayerische Motoren Werke
bn	Billion
CAM	Center of Automotive Management
CEO	Chief Executive Officer
CISG	United Nations Convention on Contracts for the International Sale of Goods
CKD	Completely Knocked Down
DIN	Deutsches Institut für Normung
EN	European Standards
EOP	End of Production
EU	European Union
EUR	Euro
EStG	Einkommensteuergesetz, German income tax law
FASB	Financial Accounting Standards Board
Field	On the road
FIN	FASB Official Interpretation of U.S.-GAAP
FRW	Free Replacement Warranty

FY	Fiscal Year
GAAP	Generally Accepted Accounting Principles
GM	General Motors Company
HGB	Handelsgesetzbuch, German code of commercial law
IAS	International Accounting Standards
IASB	International Accounting Standards Board
IATF	International Automotive Task Force
IFRS	International Financial Reporting Standards
INR	Indian Rupee
ISO	International Organization for Standardization
JV	Joint Venture
KBA	Kraftfahrt-Bundesamt
km	Kilometer
KPMG	Independent accounting firm
KRW	South Korean Won
LC	Local Currency
m	Million
M&A	Mergers and Acquisitions
MAN	Maschinenfabrik Augsburg Nürnberg
MIS	Miles in Service
MKD	Medium Knocked Down
MTBF	Mean (operating) time between failures (after repair)
MTTF	Mean time to failure
MTTFF	Mean time to first failure
MTTR	Mean time to repair
NAFTA	North American Free Trade Agreement
NHTSA	National Highway Traffic Safety Administration

OEM	Original Equipment Manufacturer
OICA	International Organization of Motor Vehicle Manufacturers
ppm	Parts per Million
ProdHaftG	Produkthaftungsgesetz – German law on product liability
PWC	PricewaterhouseCoopers
SFAS	Statement of Financial Accounting Standards, main part of U.S.-GAAP
SKD	Semi Knocked Down
SOP	Start of Production
TIS	Time in service
TTF	Total time to failure
UCC	Uniform Commercial Code
UN	United Nations
U.S.	United States
U.S.A.	United States of America
VD	Vehicle Division
VDA	Verband der Automobilindustrie – German Association of the Automotive Industry
VDI	Verein Deutscher Ingenieure – The Association of German Engineers
VW	Volkswagen

List of Figures

List of Charts

List of Tables

List of Symbols

*	multiplied
/	divided
^	to the n
€	Euro

1. Introduction

These days, the car industry is experiencing major changes. The market focus tends to be more on emerging regions with higher potential for growth.[1] A value change is taking place in the younger generation of consumers where the automobile is not as much a status symbol now as it was in previous generations. Technology wise, e-mobility is growing and will take a market share away from the traditional combustive engine technologies. Due to these changes the Original Equipment Manufacturers (OEM) have to focus more strongly than ever on their strategies for the future in order to assure their investors that they are not losing their value.

One of the important strategic factors in the automobile industry is the quality reputation of a company or the car brand[2]. In 2004, when Toyota was the third largest car manufacturer in the world, Jeffrey K. Liker wrote in The Toyota Way: "Much of Toyota's success comes from its outstanding quality reputation".[3] Today, Toyota is the biggest car manufacturer in the world. But is Toyota still the benchmark[4] when it comes to the reliability of a vehicle?[5] What would Mr. Liker say today, eight years later, seeing that Toyota's public image is affected by a high number of recalls?[6] This sensitiveness on quality issues at Toyota might be a lesson learned from the accident in 2009 in the United States of America where one woman was killed and Toyota was taken to court.[7] The aftermath of this accident led to Toyota recalling 10 million vehicles and having to pay 1.1 billion U.S. dollars[8] to rectify the problems, suspected to have been caused by a floor mat.[9]

Customers have high expectations with regards to the reliability of their vehicles. Car companies are afraid of public recall actions because this kind of publicity harms the quality reputation. The quality of the automobile as a product has a direct influence on the company's financial success, not only due to marketing factors which influence the

---

[1] Cp. ACEA (2013), pp. 75-82., OICA (2012).
[2] Cp. Hertog (2008), p. 30.
[3] Cp. Liker, J. K. (2004), p. 5.
[4] Cp. Dippe, A. (2008), p. 92.
[5] Cp. Dippe, A. (2008), p. 7.
[6] Cp. Schneider, M. C., Murphy, M. (2013) in Handelsblatt am Wochenende Nr. 221 (2013/11/15), p. 1.
[7] The court did release Toyota from the responsibility for the accident (Handelsblatt, 2013/10/11)
[8] Cp. Fasse, M. (2012) in Handelsblatt No. 250 (2012/12/28), p. 8.
[9] Cp. Fasse, M. (2012) in Handelsblatt No. 250 (2012/12/28), p. 8.

sales figures[10], but also due to costs for quality which reduce the revenue, profit and finally, the dividend payout.[11] Accumulating the warranty provisions of the three biggest car manufacturers in the world, General Motors (GM), Toyota and Volkswagen[12], the accrued amount is comparable to the budget of the German state Hesse.[13] The mentioned quality costs occur due to recall campaigns for vehicles on the road, law suits due to safety related events and warranty costs for exchange or repair caused by incapable production processes and poor design.[14] Production processes which waste less than 1 % of turnover in quality costs only are within the world class level in the electronic industry.[15] But this is not anymore an acceptable level for the car industry where the benchmark[16] failure rate of processes is supposed to be below 0.00034 %.[17] The analysis in chapter 5 will show whether this high expectation is reflected in the actual warranty figures.

The potential investor wants to know if the company in which he invests or is considering investing in, is able to generate a good profit. Most of the big OEMs are public companies listed on the important stock markets. Therefore it is possible to analyze the costs for quality using the information on provisions for warranty which is part of the annual report. This book intends to show how reliable and comparable the figure of warranty provision of OEMs in the annual report is and which valuable information the investor or analyst can get out of it. In the context of globalization, it is also important to know if there are regional differences in regards to warranty costs or provisions. In order to show as many influencing factors as possible, first the prerequisites in regards to the legal requirements and accounting rules will be shown and compared with each other. The calculation of the warranty provisions will then be explained. As the warranty payment is a future event which is not predictable at the moment when the provision is built, the calculation of costs relies on statistic models and industry specifics. Finally,

---

[10] Cp. Prabhakar Murthy, D.N., Blischke, W.R. (2006), p. 257.
[11] Cp. Kaiser, S. (2008), p. 68.
[12] Cp. General Motors Company (2013), p. 115, Toyota (2013), p. 92, Volkswagen Group (2013), p. 315, the provision also includes other items.
[13] Cp. Hessisches Ministerium der Finanzen (2011), p. 3.
[14] Cp. Prabhakar Murthy, D.N., Blischke, W.R. (2006), p. 9.
[15] Cp. Rehbehn, R. , Bülent Yurdakul, Z. (2003), p. 54.
[16] The expected capability level for processes in the automotive industry is 6 Sigma. Sigma refers to the failures which are around a defined mean in the Gaussian (normal) distribution curve. The dominant methodology used for the process improvement of manufacturing as well as administration processes in the automotive industry is the Six Sigma methodology which is also used in other industries and business areas.
[17] Cp. Levine, D. M. (2006), p. 2.

after the clarification of the prerequisites and calculation methods, the annual reports of the biggest car manufacturers will be analyzed in regards to their warranty provisions and methods of predicting the provisions for warranty.

2. Definitions

2.1 Warranty versus Guarantee

When defining warranty and guarantee, the differences are often confused.[18]

The common understanding is that the seller of a product has to warrant that his product fulfills its purpose and is free from defects.[19]

Literature about the warranty history shows that the warranty was already common practice in the twenty-first century B.C.[20] in the Assyrian and Babylonian cultures.[21] The linguistic roots of the word "warranty" can be found in old French words[22] and the German word "guarantee" but also in the Latin language from where it found its way also to other languages.[23]

If the product has a fault which negatively influences the purpose or does not meet promised specifications in a negative manner, the consumer can make a claim under warranty at the company where the product was purchased.[24] It is the responsibility of this company to repair a faulty product, to replace it or to release the buyer from the contract in the case that the failure is confirmed. In Germany this consumer right is described in § 436 in the German code of civil law (BGB). The law also defines the time period in which the product can be claimed. Since 1980 the United Nations (UN) Commission on international trade law (UNCITRAL) recommends a two year period in which the buyer can claim the product after it was handed over to him.[25] This UN statute is ratified and accepted by 79 countries.[26] The European Union (EU) Directive 1999/44EC from May 25th of 1999[27] also confirmed this period. Germany followed this

---

[18] Cp. Wawerla, M. (2008), p. 17.
[19] Cp. § 433 BGB
[20] Before Christ
[21] Cp. Prabhakar Murthy, D.N., Blischke, W.R. (2006), p. 2.
[22] Cp. Prabhakar Murthy, D.N., Blischke, W.R. (2006), p. 2.
[23] Cp. Wiewiórowska-Domagalska, A. (2013), p. 7.
[24] Cp. Alpmann-Pieper, A. (2012), p. 6.
[25] Cp. § 39 CISG
[26] Cp. Piltz, B. in NJW 35/2013, p. 2567
[27] Cp. EU DIRECTIVE 1999/44/EC OF THE EUROPEAN PARLIAMENT AND OF THE COUNCIL (2013), § 17

commandment and describes the two year period in the German code of civil law as well.[28]

In Germany, the warranty describes this right for repair, price reduction, replacement or cancellation of the purchase contract.[29] This right does not depend on the content of a contract between the seller and the buyer. It is civil law and cannot be overruled negatively for the buyer by other agreements like contracts or terms and conditions of the seller. But it can be extended favorably by voluntary guarantee contracts. Figure 2.1 shows the Guarantee from seller or manufacturer according to German law. This guarantee is independent from the warranty by law or is an extension of the warranty by law. The condition refers to the promised or expected quality within the defined duration.

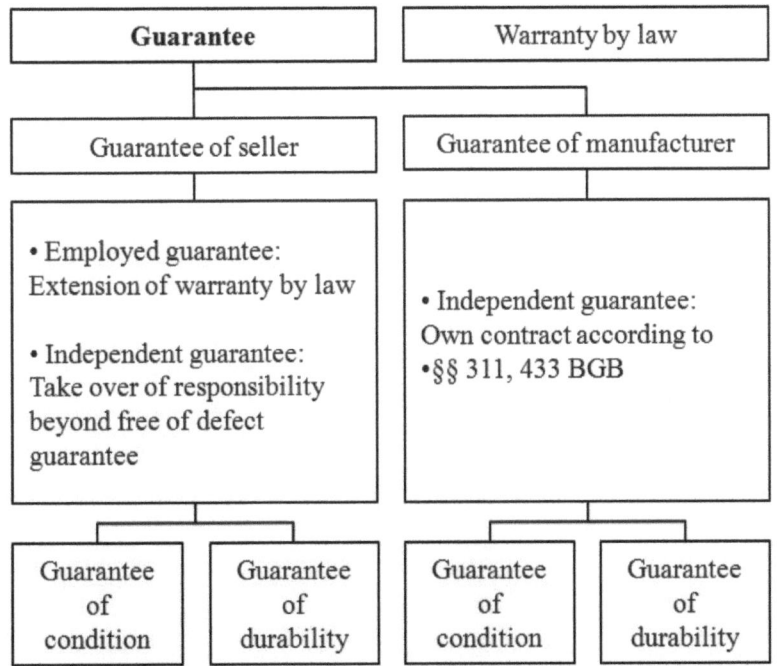

Source: Translated from Alpmann-Pieper, A. (2012), p. 65.

Figure 1: Guarantee contracts according to the German code of civil law

---

[28] Cp. § 438 BGB
[29] Cp. § 437 BGB

The warranty is a protection of the consumer by law. Which law applies, depends on the market in which the product is sold. In the United States of America (U.S.A.), which is one of the most important markets for the car business, the warranties given by law are called "implied warranties" and the voluntary guarantees are called "express warranties".[30] The implied warranty is not comparable to the warranty according to the European law, however. It does not, for example, cover a certain time period like the European law does. It only promises the product to be "fit for use" in the moment it is bought.[31] Manufacturers can bypass this law by selling the product "as is". But this disclaimer is not allowed in all states in the U.S.A.. Two warranty legislations should be mentioned in this regards. The "Magnuson-Moss Act"[32] and the "Uniform Commercial Code" (UCC)[33]. Both are federal law. The Magnuson-Moss Act is the most important warranty law in the USA and is applicable to consumer goods. The Magnuson-Moss Act requires that consumer products starting at $ 15 US are marked with "full warranty[34]" or "limited warranty" in order to improve the protection of the consumer which was not assured with the UCC.[35] Unlike German federal law, the federal Magnuson-Moss Act does not overrule the warranty law of the states.[36] The warranty period in the United States of America (U.S.A.) is defined by state law. A comparison between the guarantee periods given by the manufacturers in Germany and in the U.S.A. is shown in chart 1.

---

[30] Cp. Prabhakar Murthy, D.N., Blischke, W.R. (2006), p. 261.
[31] Cp. Prabhakar Murthy, D.N., Blischke, W.R. (2006), p. 36.
[32] Cp. Prabhakar Murthy, D.N., Blischke, W.R. (2006), p. 261. Magnuson-Moss Warranty and Federal Trade Commission Improvement Act of 1975 is commonly called "Magnuson-Moss Act".
[33] Cp. Prabhakar Murthy, D.N., Blischke, W.R. (2006), p. 261. The UCC was established by the U.S. National Conference of Commissioners on Uniform State Laws.
[34] Cp. Prabhakar Murthy, D.N., Blischke, W.R. (2006), p. 262. Full warranty means free replacement or full rebate.
[35] Cp. Prabhakar Murthy, D.N., Blischke, W.R. (2006), p. 262.
[36] Cp. Prabhakar Murthy, D.N., Blischke, W.R. (2006), p. 263.

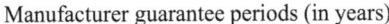

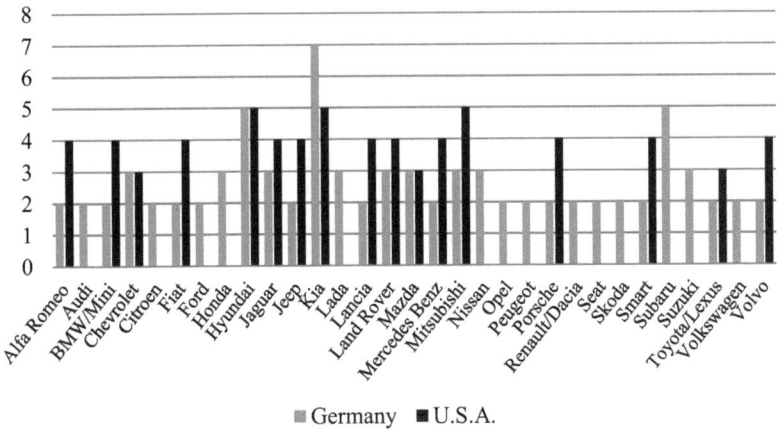

Manufacturer guarantee periods (in years)

■ Germany ■ U.S.A.

Source: Based on data from Henn, Ch. (2013) in ADAC Motorwelt No. 11-2013 p. 56.

Chart 1: Comparison of manufacturer guarantee periods in Germany and in the U.S.A.

The Chinese market is the place where the automobile business is growing out of proportion with the rest of the world. In China, repair agreements for cars are described in the vehicle-repair contract which is under control of the federal commerce administration office.[37] The period for guarantee is also defined in this contract.[38] The warranty period is defined by federal law.[39] The responsibility of the producer is comparable to that described by German law.[40] The German law on product liability (ProdHaftG) was used as an example for the definition of a nonconforming product[41] in China and the United Nations Convention on Contracts for the International Sale of Goods (CISG) is also applicable for business with China.[42]

In the car industry manufacturers often advertise their products including a voluntary "guarantee" for a certain time period or mileage and for certain parts of the vehicle. This guaranteed meeting of costs caused by certain repairs or replacements of the faulty

---

[37] Cp. Joos, B. (2013), p. 138.
[38] Cp. Joos, B. (2013), p. 208.
[39] Cp. Joos, B. (2013), p. 273.
[40] Cp. Christ, S. (2011), p. 102.
[41] Cp. Christ, S. (2011), p. 102.
[42] Cp. Christ, S. (2011), p. 99.

components of the vehicle is a voluntary extension of the legal warranty. This guarantee is defined in the written contract between seller and buyer of the car. Therefore it becomes a legal right of the buyer to claim faults which are not covered by the legal warranty.[43] The guarantee also releases the buyer from the obligation to prove that the product was already faulty at the moment of purchase, unlike the legal warranty which determines that the buyer has to prove fault within 6 months of purchase.[44] The voluntary guarantee is mainly a marketing tool which increases the quality reputation of the car brand and is supposed to strengthen the relationship between consumer and car brand.[45] Some car manufacturers offer 5 years or even more[46]. Aneta Wiewiórowska-Domagalska wrote in her dissertation about consumer sales guarantees: "The significance of the duration is based on the fact that it carries an indirect message to the consumer, how far does the guarantor stand behind the goods. This is the reason why advertisement campaigns that employ guarantees concentrate mostly on the duration of the guarantee, as the element of duration easily catches the attention of the consumer. The consumer gets the message: If somebody offers (5, 15, 100) years guarantee, the good must indeed be of an excellent quality!".[47]

Opel, which is a GM brand, received major publicity in 2010 when the Chief Executive Officer (CEO) Nick Reilly announced a life time guarantee[48] on their cars after sales dropped by 40 %.[49] At this time the Korean OEM KIA had already offered a 7 year Guarantee.[50]

Car companies did not always understand the extended guarantee as a marketing instrument but saw it also as a cost burden from which they tried to get escape. This can be seen in an EU law suit from 1983. Some Ford dealers tried to avoid guarantee services for cars which were bought in other member states of the European Union than in the one where the dealer was located. The decision of the EU Commission, referring to Article 101 refused the approach of the Ford dealers.[51] In 2010, the EU commission did strengthen the consumer rights even more and obliged the OEMs to take guarantee

---

[43] Cp. §§ 443, 477 BGB
[44] Cp. § 476 BGB
[45] Cp. Wiewiórowska-Domagalska, A. (2013), pp. 6,7.
[46] See chart 1
[47] Cp. Wiewiórowska-Domagalska, A. (2013), p. 225.
[48] Vehicle life time was defined by Opel with 160,000 km
[49] Cp. Herz, C. (2010), p. 22
[50] Cp. Herz, C. (2010), p. 22
[51] Cp. Wiewiórowska-Domagalska, A. (2013), p. 32.

responsibility also if the car was not maintained in an OEM certified dealership but in any independent garage during the guarantee period.[52]

Law cases show that the legal warranty law does not cover all circumstances. Tires, exhaust systems, bulbs or spark plugs have a lower expected life-time than the vehicle itself.[53] In Germany, purchase contracts between private buyers and a company fall under the BGB. 6 months from the day when the subject was handed over[54], the buyer has to prove that it was already faulty from the beginning.[55] The German automobile club ADAC provides a list of law suits in regards to warranty or guarantee disputes between buyers and manufacturers[56] which shows that this reversal of evidence is a reason for a high number of law suits.

No matter if the repair or exchange service is provided due to legal warranty, contractual guarantee or good will, the dealers will bill these repair to the OEM who is the manufacturer of the vehicle. These guarantees have to be covered with adequate provisions. Many components the OEMs use in their vehicles are procured from specialized companies. Therefore the OEM charges the cost for a supplier failure to the supplier of this component. This supplier will also have to build a provision for the warranty payments to the OEM and does reimburse these costs from his sub-supplier. This process does continue to the last tier[57] in the supply chain. Some OEMs deduct the expected reimbursement of suppliers from their warranty provision. Details are shown in chapter 5.

Civil law is not applicable in the case that the OEM claims the failure to his supplier. According to the German code of commerce (HGB) a company is obliged to verify the product at the moment it is handed over and has to claim a failure immediately.[58] As OEMs do not want to cover the costs for testing the incoming goods, contracts between

---

[52] Cp. EU Commission notice 2010/C 138 § 69, p. 26.
[53] Cp. VDA Volume 3.2 (2008), p. 334.
[54] Called transfer of perils
[55] Cp. § 476 BGB
[56] Cp. ADAC (2013/08/30) Liste zur Abgrenzung Mangel / Verschleiss. It contains law suits and decisions of the courts with mileage and age of the car, the defect, car brand and model.
[57] Tier is the automobile industry wording for the position of a company in the supply chain.
[58] Cp. § 377 HGB

the parties are agreed in which the quality expectations[59] are described and also the period in which the buyer can claim under warranty.

2.2 Product Responsibilities beyond the Warranty

The product manufacturer can also be made responsible for incidents which happen beyond the normal replacement or repair of his product. If it can be proven, that a failure in the product caused an accident for example, the car manufacturer is also liable for material costs and other consequences related to this accident. Especially for OEMs producing in or delivering to the United States, the risk of law suits due to the "strict liability" is higher than in other countries. Fines defined by the court[60] in the United States are higher than the penalties imposed in comparable cases in Germany. One of the reasons for this is the high compensation for immaterial damage.[61] In the ProdHaftG, it is defined who the manufacturer is and which circumstances require the liability for consequences caused by a failure of the product. According to the ProdHaftG[62], the manufacturer is not only the OEM who assembles the car, but also the manufacturers of the components of the vehicle. The definition of a failure is described in § 3 of the ProdHaftG: A product has a failure if it does not provide the safety which can be expected from its presentation, purpose of usage and the moment when it was brought into circulation.[63] The right to claim this liability from the manufacturer is limited to three years after the incident was known to the concerned complainer.[64] Ten years after the product was brought into circulation, the producer cannot be made responsible anymore.[65]

The ProdHaftG is comparable to product liability laws in other states of the European Union due to the reason that the EU Council established the directive 85/374 concerning liability for faulty products in 1985 and it has been implemented in all member states

---

[59] Quality expectations in the automotive industry are defined and measured in ppm (parts per million), DPMO (Defect Parts per one Million Opportunities) or Sigma. One failure in one million parts delivered correlates to 1 ppm or 1 DPMO. Sigma refers to the failures which are outside of a defined mean in the Gaussian distribution curve. Six Sigma, which is industry standard, correlates to a failure rate of 3.4 ppm (3,4 DPMO) or 99.9997 % good parts. Cp. Williams, M.A. (2008) p. 87.
[60] Defined by the Juries.
[61] Cp. §§ 7, 8, 9 ProdHaftG. Immaterial damage means injuries of human beings.
[62] Cp. § 4 ProdHaftG.
[63] Translation from § 3 ProdHaftG.
[64] Cp. § 12 ProdHaftG.
[65] Cp. § 13 ProdHaftG.

since then.[66] The difference between the liability of the producer responsible for a failure of his product according to the ProdHaftG and the liability of the producer according to the § 823 BGB should also be mentioned here. The liability according to the ProdHaftG is related to a failure of the product. But in § 823 BGB, the liability is related to the personal fault of harming another person, by intention or carelessness.[67] Potential risks of incidents relevant according to the ProdHaftG also have to be considered in the provisions if they fulfill the requirements for provisions mentioned in chapter 3. Recall campaigns[68] are also initiated based in the § 4 ProdHaftG[69] and § 823 I BGB.[70] The analysis in chapter 5 shows how the OEMs report these risks in the annual report.

2.3 Provision versus Accrual

Outstanding obligations of a company which will have to be paid in the future mean a certain risk for the liquidity of a business if the amount or time of the obligation is unknown. Due to that reason a provision or accrual can be created which serves as a type of reserve for an obligation in a future period. But the important difference to an actual reserve is that the amount of the provision and the accrual become a part of the liabilities. The reserve is considered part of the assets.[71]

In the annual report, the provision for warranty or guarantee is, according to the International Accounting Standards (IAS) 37.10, part of "uncertain obligations" but accruals are shown in "other liabilities" together with the accruals for pensions and tax payments.[72] Literature shows that the definition of accrual and provision is not always easily discernable. According to IAS 37.11, an accrual is used for future debits, the occurrence of which is almost confirmed and is comparable to the Statement of Financial Accounting Standards (SFAS) 5 which requests a probability of 80 % - 90 %.[73] An example for the accrual is the payment of personnel debits as vacation allowance or

---

[66] Cp. EU Council Directive 85/374/EEC.
[67] Cp. § 823 BGB.
[68] Cp. Chapter 4.3.
[69] Cp. Tamme, A. (1996), p. 13.
[70] Cp. Tamme, A. (1996), p. 14.
[71] Cp. Scheffler, E. (2011), p. 17.
[72] Cp. Melcher, W. et al. (2013), p. 34.
[73] Cp. Kaiser, S. (2008), p. 69.

Christmas bonuses.[74] Also, pending invoices for material already received from suppliers are mentioned as accruals because the uncertainty is very low.[75]

Differing from the accrual, the provision is used for future obligations which are less probable in regards to period and amount.[76] According to the International Financial Reporting Standards (IFRS) "probable" means a probability of more than 50 %[77], "possible" if the risk is lower or equal to 50 % and "remote" if it is not very probable.[78] IAS 37 says "more likely than not" and means a mathematical-statistical probability of more than 50 %.[79] The United States - Generally Accepted Accounting Principles (U.S.-GAAP) only mention "probable" as required for the creation of a provision.[80] The probability "more likely than not"[81] for provisions seems to be more adequate in regards to liabilities for warranty and guarantee due to the reason that it is very difficult to predict if a component in the car will fail during the period of warranty or guarantee. The prediction of a certain quality issue depends on statistical calculations under consideration of the technical specification of a component or system and a variety of other influences. Environmental influences like temperature or road conditions affect the reliability as well as influences of the individual driver and traffic situations. The Standard 3.2[82] of the German Association of the Automotive Industry (VDA) shows statistics of the usage which certain components in a car undergo during the lifetime of the car. For example, the standardized frequency a car's driver door is used is double that of the passenger door usage.[83] That the components of the driver's door fail earlier than the components of the passenger's doors can be statistically proven. But due to the reason that the failure statistics of components often show a stochastic behavior, that means failures occur randomly[84], long term experiences help to predict the expected warranty costs. Detailed explanations in regards to the statistical prediction of the reliability are shown in chapter 4.3.

---

[74] Cp. Melcher, W. et al. (2013), p. 34.
[75] Cp. Scheffler, E. (2009), p. 186.
[76] Cp. Melcher, W. et al. (2013), p. 34.
[77] Cp. Rothoeft, D. D. (2004), p. 97.
[78] Cp. Melcher, W. et al. (2013), p. 35.
[79] Cp. Kaiser, S. (2008), p. 70.
[80] Cp. Rothoeft,D. D. (2004), p. 98.
[81] Cp. IAS 37
[82] OEM participants: Audi, BMW, Daimler, Ford, Opel, Volkswagen, IVECO-Magirus, MAN
[83] Cp. VDA 3.2 (2008), p. 371.
[84] Cp. Precht, M. et al. (1999), p. 81.

In order to build a provision which reduces the profit and also the tax payments of a company, the probability of a warranty outflow of resources has to be calculated and documented. A stringent documentation of these calculations is of major importance[85] because it can be reviewed by the tax authorities and auditors[86] and has to be compliant with legal requirements. Building a provision is requested by local and international law and accounting standards and can differ from country to country in regards to the definitions.

If the provision is not completely used or the reason for the provision no longer exists, the provision has to be reversed partly or completely[87] and will increase the profit of the company at this moment. This adaption of the provision has to be carried out frequently or at least at the change of the fiscal year which is the closing day of the annual report.[88]

2.4 General Warranty Provision versus Specific Warranty Provision

The general warranty provision is mainly based on historical data of the OEMs warranty payments and utilization of warranty provisions during the previous years. The general provision can be characterized as a short term provision[89] which is created during the fiscal year, will be due in the actual fiscal year and was considered in the budget planning process. It is based on past experiences and reflects the calculated forecast of warranty and guarantee costs which will probably happen due to sporadic failures of components in the vehicles within the warranty or guarantee period. These general provisions are a feasible indicator for the quality level of the OEMs production process- es and quality management performance and should show a decreasing trend which, in turn indicates improvement of the quality. According to ISO/TS 16949, which is the worldwide accepted quality management certification standard for car OEMs and automotive suppliers, one of the most important tasks of the company is to maintain a quality management system which assures a continuous improvement[90] of the processes in order to guarantee customer satisfaction and to reduce costs.

---

[85] Cp. Behringer, S. (2012), p. 1.
[86] External independent Auditor of the financial reporting system.
[87] Cp. IAS 37.59
[88] Cp. Wagenhofer, A. (2013), p. 299.
[89] See chapter 2.5 Short Term Provision versus Long Term Provision
[90] Cp. International Automotive Task Force (2009), p. XIX.

Looking to the increasing trend of field recalls in Germany[91], it seems like the OEMs, which request a continuous improvement also from their tier one[92] component suppliers, have problems increasing the quality level of the complete vehicle as a system of many components delivered by different suppliers.[93] The peak of recalls in Germany was reached in 2011. Since 1998, recalls in Germany have increased from 55 documented recalls to 186 documented recalls in 2011.[94] The worldwide number of car recalls also shows an increase in this time frame. The Center of Automotive Management (CAM) published in August 2013 that recalls increased by 230 % compared to the previous year.[95]

The impact of these recalls on the warranty provisions is mainly considered in specific provisions due to the reason that major quality issues cannot be covered by the general provision due to the high unplanned cost risk. The specific provision is built immediately after the detection of the quality issue. These costs can be caused by recalls due to safety aspects or for the preventative protection of the quality reputation. In a recall, all vehicles which could be affected by a certain quality issue are called back to the dealers in order to repair or exchange the suspected faulty component. Also costs for potential law suits due to quality issues or safety related incidents can be considered in the specific warranty provision.[96] The specific provision is not planned. The quality issue cannot be foreseen but the provision will remain accrued until the issue is solved or the potential risk is not probable anymore.[97] If the risk will be present beyond the current fiscal year, a long term provision is created.[98] Annual reports show that some OEMs separate the provision for recalls from the general warranty provision and some OEMs show them together. The analysis of annual reports in chapter 5 takes a deeper look at these practices.

---

[91] Cp. Kraftfahrt-Bundesamt (2012), p. 58.

[92] Tier one = First tier supplier in supply chain, supplies directly to the OEM.

[93] Cp. Dippe, A. (2008), p. 11, refers to OESA/McKinsey Study in 2005 about the cooperation of OEM in the USA and their suppliers and Fraunhofer IAO „30 Prozent Studie" in 2003.

[94] Cp. Kraftfahrt-Bundesamt (2012), p. 58.

[95] Cp. Doll, N. (2013): Mängel am laufenden Band, in Die Welt Kompakt (2013/08/13)

[96] The Applicable law in Germany is the ProdHaftG = German law on product liability, see also chapter 2.2.

[97] Cp. Wagenhofer, A. (2013), p. 299.

[98] See also next chapter "Short Term Provision versus Long Term Provision"

IAS 37.39 also allows the combination of the general provision with the specific provision.[99] Also § 240 HGB allows the estimation of different obligations into one group provision if they are considered similar in their reason.[100]

General Provision and Specific Provision might be called differently in the companies analyzed. An average warranty cost level exists and has to be considered in the provisions, something both have in common. If major quality issues are detected which were not predictable, additional provisions are built within the fiscal year, which are related to the specific incidents. The cost risk of these incidents has to be evaluated and documented. How these costs are calculated is explained in chapter 4.

2.5 Short Term Provision versus Long Term Provision

The general provision for warranty liabilities is based on historical data and statistics and is built up at the moment when the profit was made with the sold product. This is a requirement of the accounting standards and laws which do not allow the creation of the provision if no risk exists, meaning no product was sold which could be affected by warranty.[101] The general warranty cost outflow is defined as due within the current fiscal year because the customer will request his right for immediate replacement. Therefore it is part of the short term provisions and current liabilities.

Due to the standard warranty period of several years and extended voluntary guarantees, the costs could also be due in the following years. But in order to simplify the calculation the provision is built up based on a percentage of actual sales on a frequent basis. Also specific provisions can be built up as short term provisions if the period can be estimated to be due within the current fiscal year.

Long term provisions are created for the probable warranty outflow of resources for special issues which are expected not to be due within the current fiscal year and which are part of the non-current liabilities. Long term provisions have to be discounted.[102] But standards and the tax laws do show differences regarding the percentage to be

---

[99] Cp. Melcher, W. et al. (2013), p. 112.
[100] Cp. Melcher, W. et al. (2013), p. 321.
[101] Requirements on provisions are described in chapter 3
[102] Cp. Engelberth, M. (2013), p. 13

used.[103] The adequate discount interest rate according to the German income tax law (EStG) is 5.5 %.[104] For the annual report according to § 253 HGB, the discount interest rate, which is published by the Deutsche Bundesbank[105] on a monthly basis, has to be used.[106] It is based on the average market interest rate of the previous 7 years and depends on the remaining period of the long term provision. IAS 37.47 also refers to the average market interest rate.[107] The main difference between these percentages is the consideration of the inflation in HGB and IFRS[108] which is not allowed to be applied in the report of tax relevant results according to EStG.[109]

---

[103] Cp. Behringer, S. (2011), p. 10.
[104] § 6 III EStG
[105] Available at www.bundesbank.de
[106] Cp. Melcher, W. et al. (2013), p. 130. Referring to § 253 II HGB.
[107] Cp. Wagenhofer, A. (2013), p. 298.
[108] Cp. Behringer, S. (2012). p. 4. The iBoxx corporate AA+ discount rate is a commonly used index.
[109] Cp. Behringer, S. (2011), p. 10.

3. Prerequisites on Warranty Provisions

Creating provisions requires the consideration of the applicable legal requirements. Reporting the warranty provisions has to follow the accounting principles which are the basis for general acceptance and comparability of information in the annual report. Especially in regards to the report towards the tax authorities, these principles and laws have to be taken into account. One reason that legal requirements and accounting rules are not always congruent is due to the fact that a legal requirement by law has to be followed within the country where the company has to pay its taxes. For tax and reporting purposes in Germany a company has to follow the EStG and HGB. But if the same company wants to report comparable information for its shareholders from a foreign country and other international stake holders, it has to report according to the internationally accepted reporting standards like IFRS or U.S.-GAAP because these standards are acknowledged worldwide. Compared to the HGB, which is a legal requirement, IFRS or U.S.-GAAP are known standards but not written law. Therefore, the moment a company confirms the reporting according to these official reporting standards, it can be made responsible by law if the requirements of the standards were not followed. Also local requirements are often called GAAP since this is the short form of general accepted accountings standards. Since 1st of January 2005, the IFRS is the reporting standard demanded by the EU parliament and council.[110]

3.1 Legal Requirements on Warranty Provisions in Germany

3.1.1 HGB – German Code of Commercial Law

HGB differentiates between provisions for liabilities with or without legal obligation. This has to be considered in regards to free will replacement or voluntary guarantees beyond the legal warranty. § 249 HGB allows provisions for uncertain liabilities with a legal obligation only, if the creditor is a third person according to the legal definition.[111] That means it is not a sister company, subsidiary or in other ways legally connected to the company which created the provision. The provision can only be created if the

---

[110] Cp. Regulation (EC) No 1606/2002 OF THE EUROPEAN PARLIAMENT AND OF THE COUNCIL of 19 July 2002 on the application of international accounting standards.
[111] Cp. Rothoeft, D. D. (2004), p. 54

amount of the obligation is not yet sure.[112] Furthermore, the cause for the obligation has to be present at the moment of creation of the provision.[113] That means that a real risk only exists if the products were to be sold. Due to that reason the provisions for the general warranty are created at the moment when the product is sold.

§ 249 HGB also describes the requirements for provisions for liabilities without legal obligation. These free will activities consider for example, repair and replacement of units which fail after the warranty or guarantee period or are excluded from the guarantee. The provision can be accrued as a specific provision if it is a specific issue or historical data can be used for the creation of a general provision.[114] The consumer has no legal right to this voluntary meeting of costs, but if it is common practice of the car manufacturer and part of his image in public to do this, then it must be considered in the warranty provisions.[115]

Between the tier one suppliers and OEMs, it is also current practice that the OEMs deduct costs for warranties from the tier one suppliers on a regular basis. These costs are based on actual warranty cases or calculated under consideration of the so called technical factor. In this case, the number of the claimed units in a defined region and then, multiplied by an agreed factor are considered as the worldwide failure rate. The costs for warranty are calculated based on these fictional quantities. This factor is renegotiated on a regular basis. The more accurate the documentation of claimed units at the OEM and the tier one supplier is, the more adequate the factor. But real worldwide failure quantities cannot be proven. Therefore this automotive industry practice can also be considered as good will from the tier one point of view, even it is written down in the contract between the parties.

3.1.2 EStG – German Income Tax Law

The German income tax law says that provisions can be activated in the tax relevant calculations if they are probable according to the experiences from the past. But not the

---

[112] Cp. Rothoeft, D. D. (2004), p. 55.
[113] Cp. Rothoeft, D. D. (2004), P. 54.
[114] Cp. Rothoeft, D. D. (2004), p. 56.
[115] Cp. Melcher, W. et al. (2013), p. 89.

complete amount which is deducted shall be due. The costs which have to be considered are direct and indirect costs. Long term provisions have to be discounted with 5,5 %.[116]

3.2 International Accounting Guidelines

3.2.1 IFRS – International Financial Reporting Standards

According to IAS 37, a provision is a liability where the amount and time is uncertain. For the creation of a provision IAS requires that there is firstly the future obligation from an event which took place in the past. That means a product was sold. The debtor must be a third party[117] and the obligation must be probable in regards to an event which will require the provision.[118] Here probable means that the probability for the need of the provision is higher than it is not being needed[119]. The liability of a certain component in the car is difficult to predict for each case. A car is built from thousands of components and therefore it would not be realistic to evaluate the failure probability of each component in all models. It can also be the case that some components have a very low probability of failing and other components a high probability. But it is not permitted to accrue only the case with the highest probability and to ignore the risks with a low probability.[120] Therefore it is common practice to evaluate the probability of a group of potential risks.[121] Car manufacturers also use the car models as groups for the evaluation of the probability. According to IAS 37 § 61 is it not allowed to use a provision for any other reason than the one for which the provision was created.[122]

IFRS characterizes the liabilities to be reported depending on the risk of occurrence which can be "probable" if it is more than 50 %, "possible" if the risk is lower or equal to 50% and "remote" if it is not very probable.[123] If the "possible" risk is below 50 %, it has to be characterized as a contingent liability. The provision must not be created in this case but the information has to be mentioned in the notes of the financial state-

---

[116] Cp. § 6 III EStG
[117] Cp. Buchholz, R. (2013), p. 249.
[118] Cp. Rothoeft, D. D. (2004), p. 76.
[119] Cp. Rothoeft, D. D. (2004), p. 97.
[120] Cp. Buchholz, R. (2013), p. 75.
[121] Cp. Rothoeft, D. D. (2004), p. 97.
[122] Cp. Doralt, W. (2013), p. 299.
[123] Cp. Melcher, W. et al. (2013), p. 35.

ment.[124] Due to that reason a big portion of liabilities is not considered in the balance sheet which is also a reason for the criticism on the definition of the 50 % limit.[125]

3.2.2 U.S.-GAAP – United States - Generally Accepted Accounting Principles

U.S.-GAAP requests a certain probability for provisions and requires the Management to evaluate this probability. Literature shows, that the interpretation of this definition has a wide range.[126] SFAS 5 expects that the amount of the liability can be quantified with a reliable probability.[127] Reliable probability is quantified with a range from 80 % - 90 %.[128] In the case of warranty provisions this is questionable. A provision should be built as soon as possible in order to assure the liquidity of the company. If the amount can only be quantified after the obligation is already certain and about to be due, it can be too late to build up the provision. In the official U.S.-GAAP interpretation FIN 14, the strict criteria of SFAS 5 regarding the amount was interpreted as a range of amounts[129] which is more in line with the evaluation of groups of products.

3.3 Consideration of Third Party Reimbursement

OEMs reimburse the warranty costs from the tier one suppliers if the failure was caused by the supplier. The official automotive method for this process is called "8 Disciplines" (8D).[130] The OEM claims the faulty unit to the supplier and requests the tier one to perform the 8D method[131] within an agreed time frame. The 8D method is mainly a problem solving tool but also used as report towards the customer.[132] If the supplier confirms the failure as having been caused by his fault, the claim is approved and the costs will be taken over by the supplier. IFRS[133] does not allow deducting the reimbursements of suppliers from the provisions in the balance sheet.[134] Also § 246 II 1

---

[124] Cp. Buchholz, R. (2013), p. 249.
[125] Cp. Buchholz, R. (2013), p. 249.
[126] Cp. Rothoeft, D. D. (2004), p. 76.
[127] Cp. Kaiser, S. (2008), p. 76.
[128] Cp. Kaiser, S. (2008), p. 69.
[129] Cp. Kaiser, S. (2008), p. 76
[130] Cp. VDA Volume 4 – 8D Method (2010), p. 4.
[131] Cp. Hertog (2008), p. 128.
[132] Cp. VDA Volume 4 – 8D Method (2010), p. 3.
[133] Cp. Melcher, W. et al. (2013), p. 114. C.p. IAS 37.53
[134] Cp. Rothoeft, D. D. (2004), p. 48.

HGB does not allow to deduct the third party reimbursement from the provisions.[135] But IAS gives some room for interpretation. IAS 37.54 allows considering the receivables in the total result.[136] In this case the receivables from third parties have to be shown as a separate amount.[137] This allows the analyst to get a better impression of the overall costs for warranty.

3.4 Summary of Legal Requirements and Accounting Guidelines

The major difference between the different legal requirements and accounting standards in regards to a provision is the probability of potential risks which allow them to be considered as a provision. Whether these differences have an impact on the real warranty provisions of the OEMs or not will be evaluated in chapter 5. Figure 2 shows how Rothoeft considers relevant requirements which are necessary for the recognition of a provision. As much as the probability definitions in percent vary, Rothoeft shows a very similar approach between IAS, U.S.-GAAP and HGB in the overall picture which might be due to the room for interpretation which the standards allow. That warranty costs will occur is definite. It is very unlikely that all cars sold have no warranty issue from one year to the other if they had in the past year. The question which has to be answered in regards to warranty provisions is: how high is the potential risk? This question will be examined in chapter 4. A further difference between the laws and standards, is the applicable discount rate for long term provisions. The impact is calculated with the help of examples in chapter 4. Some standards allow the deduction of supplier reimbursement. On one side this can help to see which the real quality level of the OEM is, on the other side it can lay a smoke screen onto the warranty provision if the supplier impact is not shown separately.

---

[135] Cp. Melcher, W. et al. (2013), p. 114.
[136] Cp. Wagenhofer, A. (2013), p.
[137] Cp. IAS 37.53.

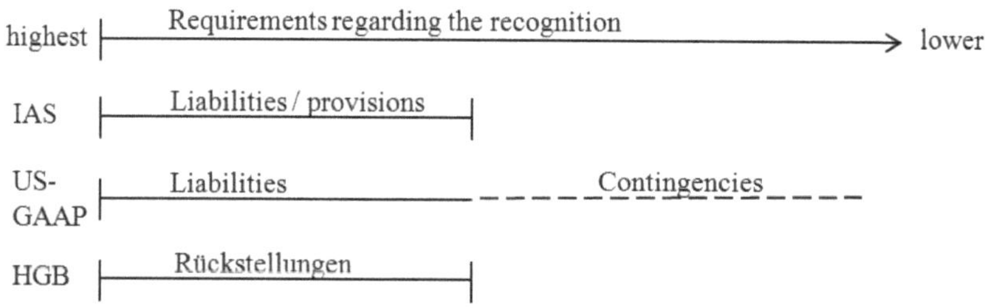

highest ├──── Requirements regarding the recognition ──────────→ lower

IAS ├──── Liabilities / provisions ──┤

US-
GAAP ├──── Liabilities ──────── _ _ _ _ _ Contingencies _ _ _ _

HGB ├──── Rückstellungen ──┤

Source: According to Rothoeft, D. D. (2004), p. 92.

Figure 2: Requirements regarding the recognition of provisions

4. Calculation of Warranty Provisions

It is of major importance to define which cost types have to be considered in the definition of the warranty provision. In the car industry, the free replacement warranty (FRW)[138] is the most common practice. The FRW includes the replacement or repair of the faulty component free of charge for the buyer.[139] The amount of the warranty provision has to correlate to the expected worst case amount[140] of the potential risk under consideration of the costs for the FRW, the maximum affected quantity and the probability of the appearance of the warranty. The worst case consideration is based on a reasonable commercial assessment[141] in order to protect the creditors of the company. But this definition also gives room for manipulation. In a law suit in the German supreme tax court (BFH) in August 2000, a company was obliged to consider the real expected amount and not the most pessimistic alternative of probable guarantee costs.[142]

The costs which have to be considered are salaries, assembly costs and the cost of spare parts, including the freight and packaging costs.[143] The manufacturer is not only responsible for the repair costs, but also for the costs for the field actions, including, amongst other things, the information of the end-user, the transfer of the car to the garage and its transfer back to the end-user after the repairs.[144]

Field actions like recalls are the most costly variant of replacement of suspected faulty products because of the high quantities and effort involved in rectifying the problems. The owners of the affected cars have to be contacted in writing by the garages or other organizations like the German Federal Office for Motor traffic, KBA[145] or the counterpart in the U.S.A., the NHTSA[146].

---

[138] Cp. Wawerla, M. (2008), p. 19.
[139] Cp. Wawerla, M. (2008), p. 19.
[140] Cp. Wawerla, M. (2008), p. 32.
[141] „kaufmännisches Vorsichtsprinzip" according to § 252 HGB
[142] Cp. Engelberth, M. (2013), p. 6. (BFH, decision from 2000/08/24 – VIII B 42/00)
[143] Cp. Wawerla, M. (2008), p. 45.
[144] Cp. Tamme, A. (1996), p. 138.
[145] Kraftfahrt-Bundesamt
[146] National Highway Traffic Safety Administration

4.1 Definitions

4.1.1 Reliability

The statistic calculation models and methods are considered as reliability engineering tools already applied during the development process of a car. Bertsche and Lechner describe reliability as the probability that a product does not fail within a defined time and under given function and environmental conditions.[147] VDA refers to a standard of the German institute for standardization, DIN[148] 55 350: "Reliability is a subset of the quality". It is the part of the quality related to the behavior within or after a defined period. Reliability emphasizes the time aspect of quality.[149]

In order to describe reliability three indications are necessary: Failure mode, wear or stress and period of operation (in mileage or time).[150] OEMs do not have a common understanding of these parameters. It is not the intention of the OEMs that all cars provide the same function, under the same conditions for the same time period. This is reflected in the (quality) image of the brand which is not necessarily in concordance to the price of the product. But all OEM have in common that their products fall under the legal warranty conditions, no matter if the car is built to last forever or built to serve other needs. That means that the gap between the real reliability and the customer expectation is covered by the warranty or guarantee.

4.1.2 Probability

The probability of the failure is the main information needed to calculate the provision. Basic probability calculations can be explained with the normal distribution curve and the definition of a mean.[151] All methods described in this chapter were developed in order to calculate the probability of the fall out behavior with limited information. Mathematical probability was already described by Laplace in 1812.[152] Laplace defined that the probability is the number of possible events divided by the number of all events.

---

[147] Cp. Bertsche, B., Lechner, G. (1999), p. 14., correlates to VDI 4001, Blatt 2
[148] DIN = Deutsches Institut für Normung e.V.. The standards are often also named DIN EN ISO which describes the harmonization on EU and international level.
[149] Cp. VDA Volume 3.1 (2000), p. 12.
[150] Cp. VDA Volume 3.1 (2000), p. 12.
[151] Cp. Sternstein, M. (1996), p. 92.
[152] Cp. VDA Volume 3.2 (2008), p. 38.

But this model based on gambling theories is not applicable when considering technical circumstances.[153] In 1931, von Mises created a probability based on tests. He used a number of random samples which had to undergo the same conditions. The fall out quantity was divided by the total quantity of samples.[154] The higher the sample quantity is, the lower the variance[155] and the more precise the result.

4.2 Calculation of the General Warranty Provision

4.2.1 Primary Financial Data

The general warranty provision is mainly based on the consideration of historical primary data of the company. Due to the reason that it is considered in the cost budget it is based on the utilization of warranty provisions of the previous years.[156] The prerequisite for the calculation is a good warranty management system. The invoices have to be booked with the correct description in order to be able to be considered in the analysis of warranty costs. It also has to be considered that not all warranty liabilities are visible as an outflow of cash or cash equivalents. Other kind of agreements could cause the equalization in the form of credits, price reductions or other kinds of compensation. The more stringent the warranty management system is, the more transparently warranty costs can be analyzed internally. The analysis is not only the basis for the calculation of the warranty provision but should also serve for the initiation of improvement in the affected product design or production and administrative processes of the company in order to reduce the costs for warranty. In the literature, some models of warranty cost calculation are described which help companies considering warranty costs in the phase of the price definition of a product and during the life cycle.[157] One thing all these methods, which are based on optimized algorithms, have in common, is that they only consider constant failure rates and repair costs.[158] The failure rates are often based on

---

[153] Cp. VDA Volume 3.2 (2008), p. 39.
[154] Cp. VDA Volume 3.2 (2008), p. 39.
[155] The variance describes the distribution around a mean. A variance of 0 is desired.
[156] Cp. Wawerla, M. (2008), p. 32.
[157] Cp. Wawerla, M. (2008), pp. 45. Refers to models of Lenz (1940), Schieke (1967), Frees (1988), Blischke, Murthy (1994), Sahin (1995).
[158] Cp. Wawerla, M. (2008), p. 48.

simulations[159] of the material or components in laboratory environments and do not reflect all impacts which exist on the road.

4.2.2 Breakdown Statistics

If no primary data can be used for the calculation of the general warranty provision, it is also possible to refer to breakdown statistics[160] which are provided by organizations like the ADAC, AVD[161], AAA[162] or other automobile researchers.

4.2.3 Calculation of the General Warranty Provision based on the Car Model

The following example considers a basic calculation of warranty provision based on Melcher et. al..[163] In the actual year the OEM launched the facelift[164] of a model which had already been on the market for three years. The historical data of warranty costs show that 3 % of net sales had to be paid in average to cover repair or replacement during the last three years. The warranty period is two years.

The first possibility is to build a provision based on the complete sales of the ongoing year until the day of the closing date. In order to simplify the calculation, the assumption is that the warranty period is two years starting from the closing date.[165] In this case sales of the ongoing year until the closing date was 6 billion EUR. The provision based on this turnover is 180 million EUR for two years.

The second method, which is more accurate, is to consider the monthly sales figures of the facelift and to calculate the general provision on a monthly basis. In months with lower sales, this can result in the reversal of parts of the provision.

---

[159] Cp. Wawerla, M. (2008), p. 48.
[160] Cp. VDA Volume 3.2 (2008), p. 140.
[161] Automobilclub von Deutschland
[162] American Automobile Association
[163] Melcher, W. et al. (2013), pp. 111, 112.
[164] Facelift is the wording for minor changes on an existing model in order to increase sales for the rest of the time in which the model is sold. Facelifts imply changes on the design or the introduction of new features.
[165] Cp. Melcher, W. et al. (2013), p. 111.

4.2.4 Calculation of the General Warranty Provision based on Components

If a new model is launched and the experiences with the warranty costs are limited, the estimation can be carried out with the warranty experiences of the components of the car because reusing of components in other models is common practice in the car manufacturing industry. Platform products are often used for different models of the same OEM.[166] For certain models, joint ventures exist between OEMs in order to reduce development costs and to increase the scale effect.[167] Therefore it is helpful to have the historical information about warranty costs on component level readily available.

The following example is based on IAS 37.39:[168] The expected sales volume of a hybrid car is 50,000 units. 60 % of the cars do not have any warranty issue at all. 20 % of the engines have problems due to software failures in the engine control unit. Cost per unit: 200 EUR. Experiences with other models show that 10 % of the batteries for the electric motor had to be replaced. Cost per unit: 5,000 EUR. 10 % of the failures are caused by different single events with an average cost of 300 EUR per unit. The calculation for the total warranty costs estimation is:

(60 % * 0 EUR + 20 % * 200 EUR + 10 % * 5,000 EUR + 10 % * 300 EUR) * 50,000
= 28,500,000 EUR.

The adequate warranty provision for the hybrid car is 28.5 million EUR.

4.3 Methods for the Calculation of the Specific Warranty Provision

The calculation of the general provision is often done by the financial departments of the company based on the existing warranty cost analysis. The calculation of specific warranty costs is mostly the responsibility of specialists for risk analysis when it comes to the estimation of the expected fall out rate of components or systems. These specialists have the statistic expertise which is needed for the prediction of future risks and the quantification of failures. The specific warranty cases harm the quality reputation of the car brand. But these incidents do not always become public. In the case that a low

---

[166] Platform strategy and reuse of components in several models also increases the risk of higher recall costs due to higher quantities on the road.
[167] The "Economies of scale" principle is based on the expectation of having lower costs due to higher quantities
[168] Cp. Melcher, W. et al. (2013), p. 113.

quantity of cars is affected by the quality issue of a component, only the owner of the car and involved stake holders know about a recall campaign. In Germany the "official recall"[169] campaigns are organized by the KBA.[170] The OEM can decide to involve the KBA or other media in the case that the quality issue has no impact on safety related concerns. If safety is compromised, the OEM is obliged to involve the KBA. The KBA database can link all cars affected by the individual failure to the owner and informs the owner in writing about the recall. In the case that the OEM decides to not involve the KBA or other media a so called "silent recall" is initiated.[171] In this case the component which is potential faulty is exchanged during the normal service. No activities are initiated at all if safety is not concerned and the fall out rate within the warranty period is low, as any special initiatives would be costlier and damage the image. In the USA, the NHTSA is responsible for recalls. Both departments, the KBA and also the NHTSA, provide information about individual recalls on their internet pages.

How negatively the image can be affected by poor quality and related recall activities can be observed in the actual press information about the biggest recall in the history of Volkswagen.[172] 2.6 Million cars had to be called back to the repair shops. Most of the affected cars were recalled due to problems with the gearbox DSG[173] in the Chinese market. This example shows that warranty provisions cannot be classified as a minor factor for the success of the company. But why was this quality issue not detected before such a high quantity of cars was sold on the Chinese market? The difficulty in detecting major failures at an early stage is that the failure has a certain behavior depending on many circumstances. If the field quality is monitored and the ppm[174] rate is within the limit of the normal stochastic fall out, no major issue is visible. The difference between normal fall out behavior and a future disaster is small at the begin-ning. Some failures appear after a few miles on the road. Other failures are detected after a certain time period or under special conditions with increased stress. Therefore the risk evaluation developed statistical methods in order to detect a major fall out as soon as possible. All of these methods have in common, that they rely on the quality of the data. The more failures are considered in the calculation, the more precise the

---

[169] Cp. Tamme, A. (1996), p. 10.
[170] Cp. Tamme, A. (1996), p. 520.
[171] Cp. Tamme, A. (1996), p. 9.
[172] Cp. Schneider, M. C., Murphy, M. (2013) in Handelsblatt am Wochenende Nr. 221 (2013/11/15), pp. 1, 8, 9.
[173] DSG = Doppelkupplungsgetriebe, the automatic transmission of Volkswagen
[174] Cp. Bertsche, B., Lechner, G. (1999), p. 33.

prediction is.[175] If the company has a good warranty management system, the chance of detecting any issue at an early stage is relatively high. If the prediction is the reaction after it was randomly detected or after it is already a publicity case, it is too late for activities geared to avoiding higher costs. In the following chapter, the methods used in the car manufacturing industry are explained in regards to the opportunities and limits these statistical methods have and if they are capable for the calculation of warranty provisions.

4.3.1 The Isochronous Diagram[176]

The Isochronous Diagram is based on field return data and the most common method for the documentation of field history in the automotive industry. The difficulty of this method is having the complete return data available. Delivery quantities and production month of the individual failed component are the basis for this method. Each failure needs to be registered with the month of its fallout. Also the time difference between the moment of sales and the registration of the car has to be considered, because the weeks or months in the warehouse or show room do not impact the wear of a component like being in use does. The diagram shows the fall out behavior of the component: the higher the peak is, the higher is the failure rate. The complete track is separated by months of production. On the left side of the horizontal x-axis is the past, which could begin with the start of production (SOP), on the very right is the current position or end of production (EOP). A horizontal line shows that the failure rate is on a constant level. If the line increases, the failure rate increases and with the production month on the x-axis it is possible to distinguish in which production month the failed unit was produced. The Isochronous Diagram does not provide a quantitative prediction of a fall out. But due to the visual overview of the past fall out behavior trends can be used as indication of the near future. If this diagram was divided into days instead of months it would also be possible to figure out if "Monday Cars"[177], or rather "lemons" really exist.

---

[175] Cp. Bertsche, B., Lechner, G. (1999), p. 35.
[176] Cp. VDA 3.2 (2008), p. 308.
[177] German phrase for a car with many quality problems from the beginning, also called lemon

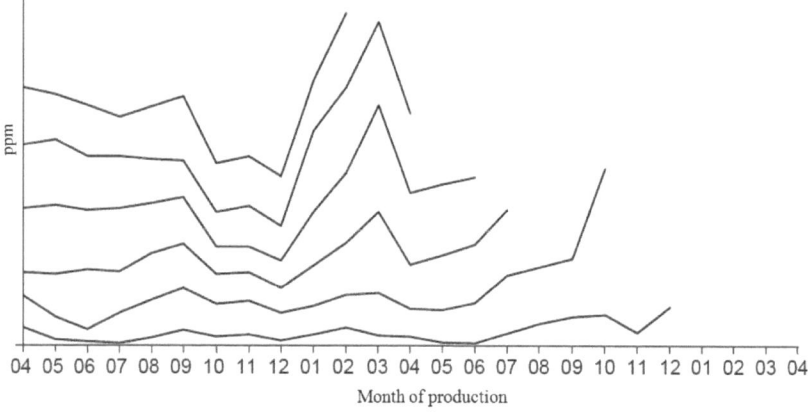

Source: According to VDA 3.2 (2008), figure 7.1, p. 308.

Figure 3: Example of an Isochronous Diagram

4.3.2 The Weibull Method

The most important method in predicting field failures in the car industry is the Weibull method.[178] It was developed in 1937[179] by the Swedish engineer and mathematic scientist Waloddi Weibull. In the automotive industry, the Weibull method is not only used for the estimation of a field events based on field return information but in the development phase of products with data from test samples or information from the literature[180]. The advantage of this method compared to other mathematical models is the consideration of the physical material characteristics. The time which characterizes the period in which the part fails, is described as mean time to failure (MTTF),[181] mean time between failures (MTBF)[182] and mean time to repair (MTTR).[183] Prerequisite for a reliable prediction of field returns according to Weibull, is the availability of failure data from the field returns history. The minimum information necessary is the production quantity or total population, quantity of failed units and remaining good units. The indicator of operation is miles in service (MIS), time in service (TIS) or the actuation

---

[178] Cp. Prabhakar Murthy, D.N., Blischke, W.R. (2006), p. 115.
[179] Published in 1951
[180] Cp. VDA Volume 3.2 (2008), p. 366.
[181] Cp. Prabhakar Murthy, D.N., Blischke, W.R. (2006), p. 101.
[182] Cp. Prabhakar Murthy, D.N., Blischke, W.R. (2006), p. 51.
[183] Cp. VDA Volume 3.2 (2008), p. 119.

according to real data or literature.[184] For the TIS it is necessary to have the registration date of the vehicle and the fall out or repair date. The MIS information results from the mileage information documented by the garage at the time of repair or exchange of the defect component.

4.3.3 The Bathtub Curve

The so called bathtub curve[185] is an outcome of the Weibull calculation and helps to categorise failures over time.[186] The curve shows an exponential[187] fall out behavior at the beginning of the life time which decreases until it is on a lower, constant level,[188] the bottom of the bathtub. If the failure rate increases again at the end of the life time it is called a bathtub curve. Production errors mainly cause failures which appear early in the life of the product.[189] These failures can be detected with end of line quality checks. If the failures are not detected it could result in a major field issue with a potential recall risk due to the high quantity. Then the "normal life period" follows which is the bottom of the bathtub. Failures happening on the bottom of the tub are random failures.[190] Increasing failures at the end of the life span are caused by mechanical wear.[191] If this increasing fall out due to mechanical wear happens within the warranty period, high warranty costs have to be expected. The voluntary guarantee contract describes which components are not subject to free replacement. Tires, brake pads, brake discs, light bulbs and spark plugs depend more than other components on individual driving and environmental conditions and have a higher wear rate resulting in shorter life spans than the expected life time of the car.[192]

---

[184] Cp. VDA Volume 3.2 (2008), p. 371 describes the actuation of components in the car
[185] Cp. VDA Volume 3.2 (2008), p. 35, p. 55.
[186] Cp. Bertsche, B., Lechner, G. (1999), p. 16.
[187] Cp. Bertsche, B., Lechner, G. (1999), p. 42.
[188] Cp. Bertsche, B., Lechner, G. (1999), p. 29.
[189] Automotive industry wording for this category is "Infant Mortality Failure"
[190] Cp. VDA Volume 3.2 (2008), p. 35
[191] Cp. Bertsche, B., Lechner, G. (1999), p. 17.
[192] Cp. VDA Volume 3.2 (2008), p. 334.

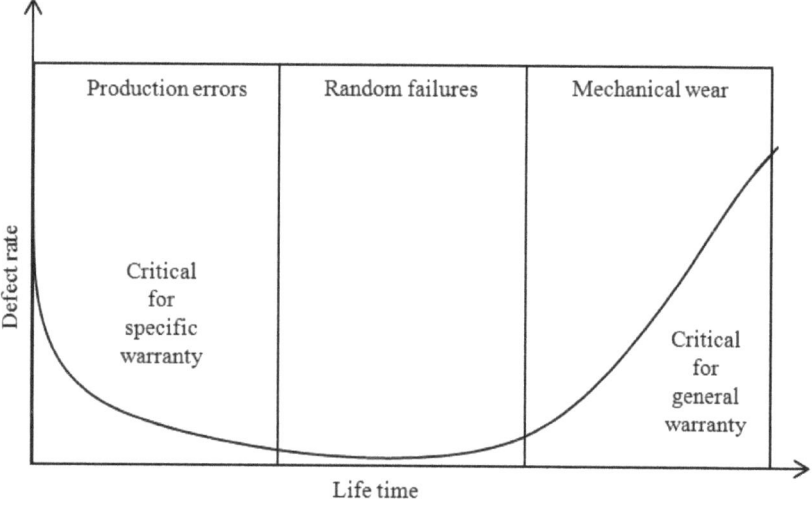

| | Production errors | Random failures | Mechanical wear |

Source: Based on VDA 3.2 (2008), figure 2.7, p. 35

Figure 4: The Bathtub Curve

4.3.4 The Sudden Death Test Method

The Sudden Death Method can also be used for components in the field.[193] The advantage of this method is that information about the quantity of good components is not needed.[194] Necessary data is the quantity of all delivered components and the number of failed parts including their operating duration in mileage or kilometer (km).[195] The failure probability in percent at the lifetime in mileage or km is the result of the calculation.[196] The tools which are used for the calculation have graphics which can be used for the interpretation of the fall out behavior. Under consideration of the guaranteed mileage or the warranty period with estimated mileage, the costs to be accrued can be calculated.

---

[193] Cp. VDA Volume 3.2 (2008), p. 323.
[194] Cp. Bertsche, B. (2008), p. 223.
[195] Cp. Bertsche, B. (2008), p. 224.
[196] Cp. Bertsche, B. (2008), p. 225.

4.3.5 The Boolean Theory

The Boolean Theory relies on the calculation with the Weibull method. It calculates the failure probability of a system of components.[197] Prerequisite is that these components are non-repairable. Besides this, only the function "operating" or "non-operating" must be available. And it is of major importance that one component does not influence the function of any other component in the system.[198]

4.3.6 The Fault Tree Analysis

The Fault Tree Analysis helps describing the failure behavior of a system based on its components and their individual failure probability. With the Boolean Theory the outcome of the Fault Tree Analysis gives a quantitative failure probability.[199]

4.3.7 The Monte-Carlo Simulation

The name of the Monte-Carlo simulation already explains the mathematical basis for this method. It is based on randomly generated numbers in order to simulate the stochastic fall out behavior of components.[200] This method can be carried out with computer software or manually using tables with random numbers. In practice the Monte-Carlo Simulation is mainly used for the estimation of spare part supply.[201]

4.4 Calculation of Collective Warranty Provisions

Collective provisions for warranties can be built if the general warranty obligation and the specific warranty obligations are based on comparable reasons. In this case, IAS 37.39 requests a sufficient number of obligations with similar amount and risk.[202]

4.4.1 Calculation of Collective Warranty Provisions for 1 Year

This example is based on IAS 37.39.[203] The car manufacturer sold 5 million cars in 2013. If each car would be affected with a general warranty issue[204] according to the

---

[197] Cp. Bertsche, B. (2008), p. 70.
[198] Cp. Bertsche, B. (2008), p. 71.
[199] Cp. Bertsche, B. (2008), p. 168
[200] Cp. VDA Volume 3.2 (2008), p. 201.
[201] Cp. VDA Volume 3.2 (2008), p. 203.
[202] Cp. Melcher, W. et al. (2013), p. 112.

historical information on average 500 EUR per vehicle, the costs to be expected are 2.5 billion EUR. If each car is affected by a specific warranty issue[205] costing 1,500 EUR, the expected costs would increase to 7.5 billion EUR. The company knows, based on its 10 year historical information, that 68 % of the sold cars have no warranty issues at all. 24 % of the sold vehicles have general warranty issues and 8 % are affected by specific warranty issues (e.g. recalls). Therefore the collective provision is calculated as follows:

(68 % of 0 EUR) + (24 % of 2.5 bn EUR) + (8 % of 7.5 bn EUR) = 1.2 bn EUR.

The adequate provision is 1.2 billion EUR.

4.4.2 Calculation of Collective Warranty Provisions for 3 Years[206]

Based on the calculation of the previous example the company has to consider the long term provisions for the complete warranty period of previous years as well.[207] The warranty period is 2 years considering an additional year for cars which are not sold immediately and remain in the show rooms or on dealer stock for one year. The assumption is, that the utilization is equal over the years and the previous years had a lower turnover which results in lower warranty provisions.

[m EUR]	Year of expected utilization			
Year of sales	2014	2015	2016	Total
2011	360			360
2012	380	380		760
2013	400	400	400	1.200
Total	1,140	780	400	**2,320**

Table 1: Calculation of collective warranty provisions for 3 years

The complete warranty provision on the fiscal year end date before tax discount is 2.32 billion EUR.

In order to be able to decide if the provision has to be discounted according to IAS 37.46[208] or § 253 II 1 HGB[209] the average mean time of the provisions has to be evaluated. The formula used for the calculation of the expected average mean time of

---

[203] Cp. Wagenhofer, A. (2013), p. 298.
[204] Within the warranty period of 3 years, considering that not all cars are immediately sold.
[205] E.g. a recall
[206] Cp. Melcher, W. et al. (2013), p. 320.
[207] Cp. Melcher, W. et al. (2013), p. 320.
[208] Cp. Wagenhofer, A. (2013), p. 298.
[209] Cp. Melcher, W. et al. (2013), p. 321.

the provisions is according to Melcher et. al.[210] the sum of the expected utilization in the partial period times the remaining periods divided by the total provision:

((1,140 m EUR * 1 year) + (780 m EUR * 2 years) + (400 m EUR * 3 years)) / 2,320 m EUR = 1.68 years. That means that the expected mean time for utilization is greater than 1 year and it is necessary to discount the provisions. The provisions have to be discounted according to the applicable laws or official discount rates.[211]

4.5 Calculation under Consideration of Inflation and Discount Rates

In order to compare the effect of the different discounting requirements, three examples follow under consideration of the requirements of IFRS, HGB and EStG. In order to simplify the examples, the assumption is that all utilizations are due at the end of the fiscal year. Results are rounded up to the third place after the point.

4.5.1 Calculation of the Warranty Provision according to IFRS[212]

The warranty provision of Table 1 in chapter 4.4.2 will be calculated according to IFRS.[213] IFRS allows the consideration of the inflation. The assumed inflation rate in this example is 1.4 % for 2014, 1.5 % for 2015 and 1.6 % for 2016.

Year 2014:

1,140 m EUR * (1 + 0.014) = 1,155.96 m EUR

Year 2015:

780 m EUR * (1 + 0.014) = 790.92 m EUR

790.92 m EUR * (1 + 0.015) = 802.784 m EUR

Year 2016:

400 m EUR * (1 + 0.014) = 405.6 m EUR

405.6 m EUR * (1 + 0.015) = 411.684 m EUR

411.684 m EUR * (1 + 0.016) = 418.271 m EUR

---

[210] Cp. Melcher, W. et al. (2013), p. 321.
[211] See also chapter 2.5 short term versus long term provision.
[212] Cp. Behringer, S. (2012), p. 4.
[213] Cp. Behringer, S. (2011), pp. 7,8

IFRS requests to use the discount rate which corresponds to the average of the market interest rates of the previous seven years.[214] The assumed interest rate of 2.94 % for this example corresponds to the iBoxx corporate AA10+ index from 2013/10/31.[215]

Year 2014: 1,155.96 m EUR / (1 + 0.0294) = 1,122.945 m EUR

Year 2015: 802.784 m EUR / (1 + 0.0294) ^2 = 757.583 m EUR

Year 2016: 418.271 m EUR / (1 + 0.0294) ^3 = 383.447 m EUR

[m EUR]	Year of expected utilization			
Year of sales	2014	2015	2016	
2011	360			Provision
2012	380	380		according to
2013	400	400	400	
Total	1,140	780	400	IFRS
+ inflation	1,155.96	802.784	418.271	
Discounted	1,122.945	757.583	383.447	**2,263.975**

Table 2: Calculation of the warranty provision according to IFRS

The discounted warranty provision according to IFRS is 2,263.975 million EUR.

4.5.2 Calculation of the Warranty Provision according to HGB[216]

HGB also allows the consideration of the inflation[217]. The calculation of the inflation is shown in chapter 4.5.1.

§ 253 II HGB requests[218] to use the discount rates of the Deutsche Bundesbank.[219] Year 2014 is discounted with 3.41 %, 2015 with 3.50 % and 2016 with 3.65 %.

Year 2014: 1,155.96 m EUR / (1 + 0.0341) = 1,117.842 m EUR

Year 2015: 802.784 m EUR / (1 + 0.035) ^2 = 749.407 m EUR

Year 2016: 418.271 m EUR / (1 + 0.0365) ^3 = 375.621 m EUR

---

[214] Cp. Behringer, S. (2012), p. 4.
[215] Cp. Mercer (2013), Verlauf des Zinssatzes 2010/2011/2012/2013
[216] Cp. Behringer, S. (2012), pp. 3,4.
[217] Cp. Behringer, S. (2011), pp. 7,8.
[218] Cp. Behringer, S. (2011), p. 8.
[219] For this example the values of October 2013 were used.

[m EUR]	Year of expected utilization			
Year of sales	2014	2015	2016	
2011	360			Provisions
2012	380	380		according to
2013	400	400	400	
Total	1,140	780	400	HGB
+ inflation	1,155.96	802.784	418.271	
Discounted	1,117.842	749.407	375.621	**2,242.870**

Table 3: Calculation of the warranty provision according to HGB

The warranty provision discounted according to HGB is 2,242.870 million EUR.

4.5.3 Calculation of the Warranty Provision according to EStG

EStG does not allow the consideration of the inflation.[220] Therefore the calculation is done with the discount rate of § 6 III EStG which is 5.5 %.

Year 2014: 1,140 m EUR / (1 + 0.055) = 1,080.569 m EUR

Year 2015: 780 m EUR / (1 + 0.055) ^2 = 700.793 m EUR

Year 2016: 400 m EUR / (1 + 0.055) ^3 = 340.645 m EUR

[m EUR]	Year of expected utilization			
Year of sales	2014	2015	2016	Provision
2011	360			
2012	380	380		according to
2013	400	400	400	EStG
Total	1,140	780	400	
Discounted	1,080.569	700.793	340.645	**2,122.007**

Table 4: Calculation of the warranty provision according to EStG

The warranty provision discounted according to EStG is 2,122.007 million EUR.

---

[220] Cp. Behringer, S. (2011), p. 9.

4.6 Summary of the Calculation of the Warranty Provision

The calculation of the general and the collective warranty provision follows a standard calculation scheme and is based on historical data of spendings for the warranty of the previous years. The difference between the highest discount rate according to EStG and the lowest discount rate according to IFRS is 141.968 m EUR. This is approximately 6 % of the provision which was originally calculated without any consideration of inflation and discount rates. This difference needs to be kept in mind comparing the individual analysis results of the OEMs with each other.

The calculation of the specific warranty provision depends on many circumstances related to technical criteria and availability of data. The application of the mentioned methods requires founded knowledge in statistical mathematics. But coming back to the main reason why a provision is created, the early prediction of the risk of a specific warranty case is of major importance for the management of a company. Considering the high amounts of costs related to the recalls of Toyota and Volkswagen is such a specific warranty issue impacting decisions which can turn for the better or take a turn for the worse of a company.

5. Analysis of the Annual Reports

In order to compare the previously evaluated prerequisites with the applied methods of the OEMs, the annual reports of the world's biggest car manufacturers were reviewed in regards to their information on warranty provisions. "Biggest" does not refer to any official ranking due to the reason that the ranking of car manufacturers can be carried out with different key figures. Some rankings show the production quantities. Other rankings consider the quantities of sold cars or turnover. Therefore, the ranking in this ana-lysis does not follow these rankings but individually compares the analyzed key figures or according to alphabetical order.

The initial question was if the data in the different reports can be compared and how valid the statement about a competitive quality level is. Due to the reason that the reported fiscal years do not always correlate to the calendar years which is mainly the case for Asian OEMs,[221] the time period reviewed is based on fiscal years 2011[222] and 2012.[223] Due to Merger and Acquisition (M&A) activities in the years 2011 and 2012, some reports cannot be compared to the previous year due to the change in the organization of the company.[224]

Firstly, all statements of the OEMs about their methods of calculating the warranty provisions are described. After that, the detailed information is compared in tables and charts. Obvious trends, anomalies or peaks are analyzed using the information of the annual reports.

5.1 Individual Statements on the Method of Warranty Provision Calculation

The individual statements of the OEMs in regard to the warranty provisions explain how the OEMs describe the method they use for the calculation of the warranty provisions in the annual report. The order is alphabetical. Due to the reason that this chapter compares the methods of the OEMs in regards to the calculation of the warranty

---

[221] Honda, Mazda, Mitsubishi, Nissan, Suzuki, TATA, Toyota. Exceptions: Korean OEMs Hyundai and KIA.
[222] 2011 Fiscal year end 31.12.2011 or 31.03.2012
[223] 2012 Fiscal year end 31.12.2012 or 31.03.2013
[224] E.g. Chrysler takeover by Fiat in 2011

provision, the described methods are cited literally from the annual reports. Tables 5 and 6 show an overview of the descriptions used and which reporting standard was applied.

BMW Group

The BMW Group, with its headquarters located in Munich, Germany, is manufacturer of cars[225] and motorcycles.[226] The consolidated financial statement was created according to IFRS and the group financial statement complies with the HGB.[227] The provisions of warranty for cars and motorcycles are not separated. The share of motorcycle sales is 6 %, which has to be considered in the financial data analysis. The provisions for warranty and guarantee are shown within the "other provisions" in the sub-category "obligations for on-going operational expenses". According to note 35[228], the major part of provisions for obligations for on-going operational expenses is caused by warranty and guarantee but an explicit warranty provision figure is not available.[229] In regards to the calculation of the warranty provisions, the BMW 2012 annual report[230] states: "Estimations are required for the purpose of recognizing and measuring provisions for guarantee and warranty obligations"[231] and furthermore says: "Various factors are taken into consideration when estimating the level of the provision, including past experience with the nature and amount of claims as well as an assessment of future potential repair and maintenance costs."[232] Specific quality issues or recalls are not mentioned by BMW. A differentiation between warranty and guarantee is made in written[233] but not reflected in the financial figures. The quality statement of BMW in regards to certain financial risks and reputation is: "The high quality of our products, which is ensured by regular quality audits and ongoing improvement measures, helps to reduce this risk. In comparison with competitors, this can rise to benefits and opportunities for the BMW group."[234]

---

[225] Automobile brands: BMW, Mini, Rolls Royce and Joint Venture (JV) BMW Brilliance
[226] Motorcycle brands: BMW and Husqvarna
[227] Cp. BMW (2013a), p. 86.
[228] Cp. BMW (2013a), p. 124.
[229] Cp. BMW (2013a), p. 124.
[230] Wording identical to 2011 report
[231] Cp. BMW (2013a), p. 95.
[232] Cp. BMW (2013a), p. 95.
[233] Cp. BMW (2013a), p. 124.
[234] Cp. BMW (2013a), p. 73.

Daimler

Daimler´s headquarters is located in Stuttgart, Germany and the company publishes the claim to be the inventor of the automobile on the first page of the annual report.[235] Daimler manufactures cars[236] and commercial vehicles like vans,[237] busses[238] and trucks.[239] Daimler also reports the annual financial statements according to HGB and follows IFRS for the consolidated financial statements.[240] It is mentioned that provisions show differences between these standards.[241] If this concerns warranty provisions, will be shown in the financial data analysis. The warranty provisions are not separated by divisions. That means that it has to be considered that warranty estimates include all types of vehicles from a Smart car via the S-Class up to a truck. The provisions for warranty are shown within the "provisions for other risks", divided into current and non-current provisions.[242] Daimler describes the method for the calculation of warranty provisions briefly: "Estimates for accrued warranty costs are primarily based on historical experiences."[243] On the next page, Daimler explains warranty estimates in more detail: "Based on historical warranty claim experience, assumptions have to be made on the type and extent of future warranty claims and customer goodwill, as well as on possible recall or buyback campaigns for each model series. In addition, the estimates also include assumptions on the amounts of potential repair costs per vehicle and the effects of possible mileage limits. The provisions are regularly adjusted to reflect new information."[244] Finally the estimation of warranty and guarantee is explained under the chapter "provisions for other risks": The provision for these product warranties covers expected costs for legal and contractual warranty claims, as well as expected costs for policy coverage, recall campaigns and buyback commitments."[245] Non-current provisions for warranty from products sold in 2012 consider warranty obligations until 2015.[246] Daimler also included a quality statement into the report: "Product quality has a major influence on a customer´s decision to buy a car or a

---

[235] Cp. Daimler (2013), p. 1.
[236] Brands: Mercedes-Benz, Smart
[237] Brands: Mercedes-Benz, Freightliner
[238] Brands: Mercedes-Benz, Setra
[239] Brands: Mercedes-Benz, Freightliner, Fuso, Western Star, Thomas, BharatBenz
[240] Cp. Daimler (2013), p. 114.
[241] Cp. Daimler (2013), p. 114.
[242] Cp. Daimler (2013), p. 237.
[243] Cp. Daimler (2013), p. 206.
[244] Cp. Daimler (2013), p. 207.
[245] Cp. Daimler (2013), p. 236.
[246] Cp. Daimler (2013), p. 236.

commercial vehicle"[247] and closes with: "Technical problems could lead to recall and repair campaigns, or could even necessitate new engineering work. Furthermore, deteriorating product quality can lead to higher warranty and goodwill costs."[248] Daimler explains the higher profit in the car business in 2011 also with lower costs for warranty.[249] In 2012 this was the case for trucks and vans but not for the car division.[250]

Fiat Group

The Italian Fiat Group is a manufacturer of cars and light commercial vehicles.[251] Chrysler was taken over by Fiat in 2011. Some financial data is separated into Fiat with Chrysler and Fiat without Chrysler. The warranty provision information in the annual reports of 2011 and 2012 are not separated. Therefore the figures of 2011 and 2012 cannot be compared with each other. The method for the calculation of warranty cost provisions is described as follows: "The estimate of the provision is based on historical information concerning the nature, frequency and average cost of warranty claims."[252] Warranty provisions are shown under the "other provisions".[253] Under other provisions the explanation is: "The warranty provision represents the best estimate of commitments given by the Group for contractual, legal or constructive obligations arising from product warranties given for a specified period of time beginning at the date of sale to the end customer. This estimate is principally based on assumptions regarding the lifetime warranty costs of each vehicle and each model year of that vehicle line, as well as historical claims experiences for our vehicles. The provision also includes management's best estimate of the costs that are expected to be incurred in connection with product defects that could result in a general recall of vehicles, which is estimated by making an assessment of the historical occurrence of defects on a case-by-case basis".[254] The quality statement of the Fiat Group in regards to warranty costs is: "The Group seeks to improve vehicle quality and minimise warranty expenses arising from claims."[255]

---

[247] Cp. Daimler (2013), p. 129.
[248] Cp. Daimler (2013), p. 129.
[249] Cp. Daimler (2012), p. 90.
[250] Cp. Daimler (2013), p. 93.
[251] Brands: Fiat, Alfa Romeo, Lancia, Abarth, Chrysler, Jeep, Dodge, RAM, SRT, Ferrari, Maserati.
[252] Cp. Fiat Group (2013), p. 117.
[253] Cp. Fiat Group (2013), p. 168.
[254] Cp. Fiat Group (2013), p. 168.
[255] Cp. Fiat Group (2013), p. 117.

Ford Motor Company

The Ford Motor Company is one of the automobile players[256] located in the area of Detroit, U.S.A., and produces a variety of cars and light trucks. Ford sold the Jaguar and Land Rover brands to TATA recently. Ford shows warranty and recall cost provision in one figure using the word "accrual" instead of "provision". Beside warranty and recall, the "customer satisfaction actions"[257] are also included. The methods for the calculation are explained as follows: "We establish estimates using historical information regarding the nature, frequency, and average cost of claims for each vehicle line by model year. Where little or no claims experiences exists, we rely on historical averages."[258]... "Product recalls are distinguishable from warranty coverages in that the actions may extend beyond basic warranty coverage periods." Ford also describes the process: "We reevaluate our estimates of warranty obligations on a regular basis. Experience has shown that initial data for any given model year may be volatile; therefore, our process relies on long-term historical averages until sufficient data are available. As actual experience becomes available, we use data to modify the historical averages in order to ensure that the estimate is within the range of likely outcomes. We then compare the resulting accrual with present spending rates to ensure that the balances are adequate to meet expected future obligations."[259] Concerning quality, Ford has an official metric called "Quality" which is published in the annual report.[260]

General Motors Company

GM headquarters is also located in Detroit, U.S.A. GM is one of the biggest car manufacturers in the world but was hit hard by the economic crisis and went through a chapter 11[261] in 2009. GM produces cars and light commercial vehicles.[262] GM reports the warranty provisions separated by current accrued liabilities and non-current other liabilities. They include also the recall campaigns and mention the warranty also for used vehicle sales.[263] The method for the warranty provision calculation including a quality statement is described as follows: "These estimates are established using

---

[256] Beside General Motors and Chrysler
[257] Cp. Ford (2013), p. 11.
[258] Cp. Ford (2013), p. 51.
[259] Cp. Ford (2013), p. 51.
[260] Cp. Ford (2012), p. 47.
[261] Chapter 11 is a title from the USA Bankruptcy Code
[262] Cp. Brands: Buick, Cadillac, Chevrolet, GMC, Holden, Opel, Vauxhall, Alpheon, Baojun, Jiefang, Wuling
[263] Cp. GM (2013), p. 115.

historical information on the nature, frequency and average cost of claims of each vehicle line or each model year of the vehicle line and assumptions about future activity and events. Revisions are made when necessary, based on changes in these factors. Trends of claims are actively studied and actions are taken to improve vehicle quality and minimize claims. The estimated costs related to product recalls are based on a formal campaign soliciting return of that product are accrued when they are deemed to be probable and can be reasonably estimated."[264] Recall campaigns are not mentioned in detail.

Honda Motor Company

Honda is a Japanese car and motorcycle manufacturer located in Tokyo. Car and motorcycle financial data of provisions for warranty are not separated. In 2012 the Motorcycle turnover was 14 % of total sales and car sale was 78 %.[265] Honda explicitly shows the warranty provision separated from other kinds of provisions[266] and explains the method: "Product warranties vary depending upon the nature of the product, the geographic location of their sales and other factors. We recognize costs on general warranty on products we sell and product recalls…Estimated warranty costs are provided based on historical warranty claim experience with consideration given to the expected level of future warranty costs, including current sales trends, the expected number of units to be affected and the estimated average repair cost per unit for warranty claims."[267] The following statement needs to be reviewed in more detail: "Our products contain certain parts manufactured by third party suppliers. Since suppliers typically warrant these parts, the expected receivables are deducted from our estimates of accrued warranty obligation."[268] Honda reports according to U.S.-GAAP. Literature points out that this method is not allowed according to IAS[269]. But IAS 37 also describes exceptions from this general rule. IAS 37.54 allows deducting these supplier receivables in the statement of income and accumulated earn.[270] IAS 37.53 says that it has to be shown as a separate amount.[271] Honda is responsible for the complete amount

---

[264] Cp. GM (2013), p. 85.
[265] Cp. Honda (2013), p. 12.
[266] Cp. Honda (2013), p. 40.
[267] Cp. Honda (2013), p. 40.
[268] Cp. Honda (2013), p. 40.
[269] Cp. Rothoeft, D. D. (2004), p. 48.
[270] Cp. Wagenhofer, A. (2013), p. 299.
[271] Cp. Wagenhofer, A. (2013), p. 299.

if the supplier is not willing to pay or cannot pay.[272] IAS 37.56 mentions that the company is liable for the amount if no other party will be and therefore the provision as well as the expected reimbursement have to be reported separately.

Hyundai Motor Company

Hyundai is a Korean car and motorcycle manufacturer located in Seoul with the car brands Hyundai and KIA. Hyundai also works in the steel and construction industries. Some of the financial figures in the annual reports are shown according to Korean-GAAP[273] and Korean-IFRS[274] due to the reason that Hyundai just started to report according to the Korean-IFRS in 2011.[275] The method for the calculation of warranty provisions is described as follows: "The Group generally provides a warranty to the ultimate consumer for each product sold and accrues warranty expenses at the time of sale based on actual claims history. Also, the Group accrues probable expenses, which may occur due to product liability suit, voluntary recall campaign and other obligations at the end of the reporting period."[276] Warranty provisions are not separated by current or non-current provision. Also Hyundai deducts the expected reimbursement from suppliers from the warranty provisions.[277] Unlike Honda, the expected receivables from suppliers are shown separately, in line with IAS 37[278]: "When some or all of the economic benefits required to settle a provision are expected to be recovered from a third party, a receivable is recognized as an asset if it is certain that reimbursement will be received and the amount of the receivable can be measured reliably."[279] KIA Motors reports the supplier receivables the following way: "Where some or all of the expenditures required to settle a provision are expected to be reimbursed by another party, the reimbursement shall be recognized when, and only when, it is virtually certain that reimbursement will be received if the entity settles the obligation. The reimbursement is treated as a separate asset. "[280]

---

[272] Cp. Wagenhofer, A. (2013), p. 299.
[273] Cp. Korea GAAP
[274] Cp. Korea IFRS
[275] Cp. Hyundai (2013), p. 8.
[276] Cp. Hyundai (2013), p. 94.
[277] Cp. Hyundai (2013), p. 115.
[278] See Honda statement
[279] Cp. Hyundai (2013), p. 94.
[280] Cp. KIA (2013), p. 65.

Mazda Motor Corporation

Mazda is a Japanese car manufacturer from Hiroshima. Mazda utilizes the word "reserves"[281] for warranty liabilities which is uncommon[282] because reserves in the common meaning are not part of the liabilities.[283] The different wording might be explained with the fact that Mazda reports according to Japanese GAAP. Warranty provisions are shown in current-liabilities only,[284] which is very similar to Nissan.[285] Under the chapter "Reserve for Warranty Expenses" Mazda mentions: "In order to match the recognition of after-sales expenses to product (vehicle) sales revenues, an amount estimated based on product warranty provisions and actual costs incurred in the past, taking future prospects into consideration, is recognized."[286]

Mitsubishi Motors Corporation

The Japanese Mitsubishi Motors Corporation is part of the Machinery Group within the Mitsubishi Corporation. Mitsubishi reports according to U.S.-GAAP. The statement about warranty provisions is short: "Certain subsidiaries accrue estimated product warranty cost, in relation to their sales of products, to provide for warranty claims."[287]

Nissan Motor Company

The Japanese Nissan Motor Company has a close alliance with Renault. Nissan is a manufacturer of cars[288] and commercial vehicles. Warranty provisions are separately shown within the current- and the long-term liabilities.[289] An explanation of the used method for the calculation of warranty provisions was not available.

PSA Peugeot Citroën

PSA is a French manufacturer of cars and light commercial vehicles with headquarters in Paris. PSA is suffering from the recession especially in the markets in the southern part of Europe.[290] The company explains the warranty provision calculation method as follows: "The provision for warranties mainly concerns sales of new vehicles, where the contractual obligations cover generally two years. It correspondents to the expected cost

---

[281] Cp. Mazda (2013), p. 33.
[282] See also chapter 2.3. Provision versus Accrual.
[283] Cp. Scheffler, E. (2011), p. 17.
[284] Cp. Mazda (2013), p. 33.
[285] Cp. Nissan (2013), p. 27.
[286] Cp. Mazda (2013), p. 39.
[287] Cp. Mitsubishi (2013b), p. 139.
[288] Brands: Nissan, Infiniti and Datsun
[289] Cp. Nissan (2013a), p. 27.
[290] Cp. PSA (2013), p. 18.

of warranty claims related to vehicles and replacement parts."[291] The favorable change in warranty provisions is explicitly explained and will be analyzed in detail in chapter 5.3.5: "The decline in warranty costs resulting from improvements to vehicle quality led to a € 71 million reduction in the related provisions in 2012 (€ 210 million reduction in 2011)".[292] The trend of the warranty provisions between 2006 and 2012 is shown in charts 8 and 9. PSA also mentions the reimbursement of suppliers but does not deduct it from the provisions:"The amount expected to be recovered from suppliers is recognised as an asset under "Miscellaneous other receivables"(Note 24)."[293]

Renault

Renault is a French car and commercial vehicles manufacturer.[294] The statement about warranty provisions is: "Provisions for costs to be borne by Renault are valued on the basis of observed data by model and engine, i.e. the level of costs, and their distribution over the periods covered by the manufacturer's warranty. In the event of product recalls relating to incidents that come to light after the vehicle has been put on the market, provisions are established to cover the costs involved as soon as the decision to under-take the recall campaign has been made."[295] Renault also deducts supplier reimburse-ments from the warranty provision: "Amounts claimed from suppliers are deducted from the warranty expenses when it is considered practically certain they will be recovered."[296]

Suzuki Motor Corporation

Suzuki is a Japanese car and motorcycle manufacturer. Even considering that produc-tion quantities of motorbikes and cars are on a comparable level,[297] the share on net sales of the automobile business is 89.1 %. The explanation in regards to the warranty provisions is: "The provision is appropriated into this account based on the warranty agreement and past experiences in order to allow for expenses related to the mainte-nance service of products sold."[298] Quantitative figures of warranty provisions are not shown.

---

[291] Cp. PSA (2013), p. 84.
[292] Cp. PSA (2013), p. 85.
[293] Cp. PSA (2013), p. 84.
[294] Brands: Renault, Dacia, RSM and joint ventures with Avtovaz, Nissan, Volvo and Daimler.
[295] Cp. Renault (2013c), p. 19.
[296] Cp. Renault (2013c), p. 19.
[297] Cp. Suzuki (2013), p. 5. (motorcycle production quantities are 44 % but sales share is only 8.9 %)
[298] Cp. Suzuki (2013), p. 38.

Subaru

Subaru is a car manufacturer specialized on all wheel drive and belonging to the Japanese Fuji Heavy Industries group. The statement in the annual report about warranty provisions is: "The Company and its consolidated subsidiaries provide for accrued claims on products sold based on their past experiences of warranty services and estimated future warranty costs, which are included in "accrued expenses" in the accompanying consolidated balance sheets."[299]

TATA Motors

TATA Motors is the only Indian OEM in this analysis and well known as the inventor of the low price TATA Nano. TATA manufactures cars and commercial vehicles. TATA emerged as one of the big players in the global automobile business taking over Jaguar and Land Rover and is the 4th largest bus and 5th largest truck manufacturer in the world[300] with consolidated revenue of approximately 22.8 billion EUR. The annual report of TATA is a mixture of different reporting standards, depending on the brand or company. IFRS is used for Jaguar and Land Rover[301] and Korean GAAP is used for Korean companies.[302] The overall reporting standard applied is not visible. Warranty provisions are shown within long term provisions[303] and short term provisions.[304] TATA mentions that warranty provisions did increase mainly due to Jaguar and Land Rover volumes.[305] The explanation for the warranty provision calculation is described two times with a difference in the warranty period. The first explanation in the "Standalone financial statements" says: "These estimates are established using historical information on the nature, frequency and average cost of warranty claims and management estimates regarding possible future incidents based on corrective actions on product failures. The timing of outflows will vary as and when warranty claim will arise – being typically up to 3 to 4 years."[306] Later on the same explanation is used in the "Consolidated financial statements" with a longer warranty period: "… being typically upto five years."[307]

---

[299] Cp. Subaru (2013), p. 3.
[300] Cp. TATA (2013), p. 13.
[301] Cp. TATA (2013), p. 53.
[302] Cp. TATA (2013), p. 48.
[303] Cp. TATA (2013), p. 135, p. 180.
[304] Cp. TATA (2013), p. 136, p. 180.
[305] Cp. TATA (2013), p. 76.
[306] Cp. TATA (2013), p. 126.
[307] Cp. TATA (2013), p. 169.

Toyota Motor Corporation

Toyota is competing with Volkswagen and GM to be the number one car manufacturer in the world. Toyota is a car and light commercial vehicle manufacturer[308] with its headquarters located in Tokyo. Toyota reports according to U.S.-GAAP. Toyota shows warranty provisions within "liabilities for quality assurance" which are also included in the "accrued expenses" in the consolidated balance sheet.[309] Recalls and other safety measures are reported separately. The method for the estimation of warranty provisions is explained as follows: "Toyota accrues for costs of recalls and other safety measures at the time of vehicle sale based on the amount estimated from historical experience."[310] Toyota uses a whole page explaining the method and further details regarding the calculation of the general warranty, recalls and other quality related provisions. The used cost figures for example depend on the geographical region based on the past 10 years. Toyota also uses a "pattern of payment occurrence" which is as well based on a 10 years history.[311] Furthermore the reimbursement of suppliers is also mentioned: "The amount of warranty costs accrued also contains an estimate of warranty claim recoveries to be received from suppliers."[312] Toyota also mentions the major recalls which did affect the company also including the aforementioned floor mat issue.[313]

Volkswagen Group

Volkswagen (VW) the biggest German car, motorcycle and commercial vehicle manufacturer[314] is one of the three biggest car manufacturers in the world. Like the other two German OEMs in this analysis, also Volkswagen follows the IFRS and HGB reporting rules. The auditor states that differences in the provisions exist between both standards.[315] Similar to BMW, the Volkswagen Group reports warranty provisions below "other provisions"[316] which does not provide a reliable transparency in regards to warranty costs for the analyst even though it is mentioned that these other provisions primarily contain warranty provisions.[317] Only the Volkswagen AG report according to

---

[308] Brands: Toyota, Lexus, Daihatsu, Hino
[309] Cp. Toyota (2013), p. 92.
[310] Cp. Toyota (2013), p. 92.
[311] Cp. Toyota (2013), p. 68.
[312] Cp. Toyota (2013), p. 68.
[313] Cp. Toyota (2013), p. 47, p. 109.
[314] Brands: VW, Porsche, Audi, Bugatti, Lamborghini, Ducati, Skoda, Seat, Bentley, Porsche, Scania, MAN
[315] Cp. Volkswagen (2013a), p. 353.
[316] Cp. Volkswagen (2013a), p. 315.
[317] Cp. Volkswagen (2013a), p. 316.

HGB provides a figure of warranty provisions. The warranty estimation is described as follows: "Warranty claims from sales transactions are calculated on the basis of losses to date, estimated future losses and the policy on ex gratia[318] arrangements."[319]

Volvo - Geely Sweden AB

The Volvo car group is owned by the Chinese group Geely. The warranty method is explained as follows: "The initial calculations of the reserves are based on historical warranty statistics considering known quality improvements, costs for remedy of defaults etc."[320] …"Warranty provisions are estimated based on historical claims statistics and the warranty period.".…"Refunds from suppliers that decrease Volvo Car Group´s warranty costs are recognised to the extent these are considered to be virtually certain."[321]

5.2 Summary of the Statements

Most of the statements on the methods for the calculation of warranty provisions are identical in content, some are even identical in the wording. All have in common that the provisions are based on estimates and history. Certain OEMs even estimate expected recall costs based on historical experiences. The names of statistical methods are not mentioned. Toyota provides the most detailed information about the calculation method and also some numbers like the years of history on which the estimation is based and details about recall campaigns. Some OEMs deduct expected supplier refunds from their warranty provision, partly shown explicitly and partly not shown at all. In the following analysis of the warranty provisions compared to sales or number of units, it has to be considered that some companies have a portfolio of cars, motorcycles and trucks or other business segments but the warranty provisions are not separated according to individual divisions in most of the cases. Due to that, the assumption is that a more expensive vehicle also has higher warranty costs. That means that the overall figure should be balanced in regards to warranty provision compared to sales. The used reporting standards depend on the geographical region of the OEM´s headquarters. The

---

[318] Ex gratia is the legal expression for "voluntary", in this case voluntary guarantee or good will.
[319] Cp. Volkswagen (2013a), p. 280.
[320] Cp. Volvo-Geely Sweden (2013), p. 15.
[321] Cp. Volvo-Geely Sweden (2013), p. 17.

European OEMs follow the EU regulation from 2002[322] and report according to IFRS. American and Asian OEMs report according to GAAP. Tables 5 and 6 show a summary of significant details of the analyzed annual reports.

OEM	Warranty provision reported as	Warranty provision in balance sheet reported under	Reporting Standard
BMW AG	Prevention for obligations from guarantee*	Other provisions	HGB
BMW Group	Obligations for ongoing operational expenses*	Other provisions	IFRS
Daimler AG	No information	No information	HGB
Daimler Group	Product warranties	Provisions for other risks	IFRS
Fiat	Warranty provision	Other provisions	IFRS
Ford	Warranty accruals	Accrued liabilities	U.S. GAAP
GM	Policy, product warranty and recall campaigns	Accrued/other liabilities	U.S. GAAP
Honda	Provisions for product warranties	Accrued expenses	U.S. GAAP
Hyundai	Warranty	Provisions	Korean IFRS
KIA	Provision of warranty for sale	Provisions	Korean IFRS
Mazda	Reserve for warranty exenses	Reserve for warranty expenses	Japanese GAAP
Mitsubishi	Allowance for product warranties	Accounts payable, other and accrued expenses	U.S. GAAP
Nissan	Accrued warranty costs	Accrued warranty costs	IFRS
PSA	Warranties	Current provisions	IFRS
Renault	Provisions for warranty costs	Provisions	IFRS
Subaru	Provision for product warranties	Provision for product warranties	Japanese GAAP
Suzuki	No information	No information	Japanese GAAP
TATA	Provision for warranty	Long term Provisions, current liabilities	India GAAP
Toyota	Liabilities for quality assurances	Accrued expenses	U.S. GAAP
VW AG	other provisions	Provisions	HGB
VW Group	Obligations arising from sales*	Other provisions	IFRS
Volvo Geely AB	Warranties	Current and other non-current provisions	IFRS
* includes also other items			

Table 5: Descriptions of warranty provisions in annual reports

---

[322] Cp. Regulation (EC) No 1606/2002 OF THE EUROPEAN PARLIAMENT AND OF THE COUNCIL of 19 July 2002 on the application of international accounting standards.

OEM	Explicit quantitative figures about warranty provisions available in annual report	Statement about method of calculation of the warranty provision available	Warranty provision including recall / product liability	Third party (Supplier) reimbursement deducted from warranty provision	Reporting Standard
BMW AG	no	no	yes	no information	HGB
BMW Group	no	yes	seperately	no information	IFRS
Daimler AG	no	no	no information	no information	HGB
Daimler Group	yes	yes	yes	seperately	IFRS
Fiat	yes	yes	yes	no information	IFRS
Ford	yes	yes	yes	no information	U.S. GAAP
GM	yes	yes	yes	no information	U.S. GAAP
Honda	yes	yes	yes	yes	U.S. GAAP
Hyundai	yes	yes	yes	yes	Korean IFRS
KIA	yes	yes	yes	seperately	Korean IFRS
Mazda	yes	yes	no information	no information	Japanese GAAP
Mitsubishi	yes	yes	no information	no information	U.S. GAAP
Nissan	yes	no	no information	no information	IFRS
PSA	yes	yes	no information	seperately	IFRS
Renault	yes	yes	yes	yes	IFRS
Subaru	yes	yes	no information	no information	Japanese GAAP
Suzuki	no	yes	no information	no information	Japanese GAAP
TATA	yes	yes	yes	yes	India GAAP
Toyota	yes	yes	seperately	yes	U.S. GAAP
VW AG	yes	yes	no information	no information	HGB
VW Group	no	yes	no information	no	IFRS
Volvo Geely AB	yes	yes	yes	yes	IFRS

Table 6: Content in regards to warranty provisions in annual reports

5.3 Financial Data Analysis

The analysis of the financial data considers the information as presented in the annual reports. Comparisons between the OEMs with other local currencies (LC) than EUR were calculated to the EUR currency based on the exchange rate[323] on the fiscal year end date[324] of the annual report. Figures of sold units comprise complete vehicles and depending on the OEM also completely (CKD), semi (SKD) or medium-knocked down units (MKD).[325] Sales figures are related to the automotive sales without other businesses or services whenever the information was available separately.

Literature shows different possibilities to calculate provision ratios[326] in order to analyze the economic situation of a company. The reason for this analysis is to compare the methods of the calculations of warranty provisions. Due to the reason that the

---

[323] Exchange rate according to OANDA
[324] 31.12. or 31.03. depending on the fiscal year of the OEM.
[325] "Knocked down" is the expression for vehicles which are sold as components for later assembly.
[326] Cp. Scheffler, E. (2011), p. 41.

warranty provision is based on sales of vehicles sold, the ratios in this analysis are calculated with warranty provision in percentage of sales and warranty provision per vehicle sold. As guarantee and warranty are shown as one figure in the annual reports, warranty is used in this analysis but in fact means both warranty and guarantee.

5.3.1 Comparison of Warranty Provisions in Percent of Sales

The annual reports of the car manufacturers were analyzed in regard to their warranty provision in percentage of sales. The annual reports of BMW, Daimler, Suzuki and the Volkswagen Group[327] did not show figures explicitly for warranty or guarantee but also include other items.[328] Chart 2 compares the provisions in percent of sales.

The values vary between 1,3 % (Mazda, FY 2012/2013) and 5,7 % (Hyundai, FY 2012). With the information of the annual reports, some interpretations can explain changes between 2011 and 2012 or differences between the companies. It is visible that most of the companies show a decrease in 2012 compared to 2011. Hyundai shows the highest amount in 2012. In chart 1, it is visible that Hyundai offers 5 year guarantee and Kia, which belongs to Hyundai, up to 7 years. This could be a reason for the high warranty provision. Fiat shows a significant decrease from 2011 to 2012. The reason is that Chrysler was included into the annual report of Fiat starting June 2011[329]. Therefore the 2011 sales figures are lower than in 2012. The warranty provision of Fiat increased slightly.[330] An explanation for Mazda's low level of warranty provisions could be the fact, that only short term provisions are reported as warranty provision and long term is not considered as warranty[331]. The two competitors in regards to place number one as biggest car manufacturer, Toyota and Volkswagen[332] show a very similar level in the last two years. In charts 6 and 7 these two competitors are compared for a period of 6 years in order to take a deeper look into the history. Also the two French companies which show a serious decrease in sales due to the suffering European car market, PSA and Renault are compared with each other over a period of the last 6 years in charts 8 and 9. A significant difference between the reporting standards IFRS, U.S.-GAAP and

---

[327] The annual report of the Volkswagen AG does explicitly show warranty provisions.
[328] Therefore marked with a star
[329] Cp. Fiat (2013), p. 4.
[330] Cp. Fiat (2013), p. 168.
[331] Cp. Mazda (2013), p. 33.
[332] Volkswagen AG annual report according to HGB

HGB is not visible.[333] Charts 4 and 5 compare the figures of Volkswagen according to IFRS[334] and HGB[335] during the last 6 years.

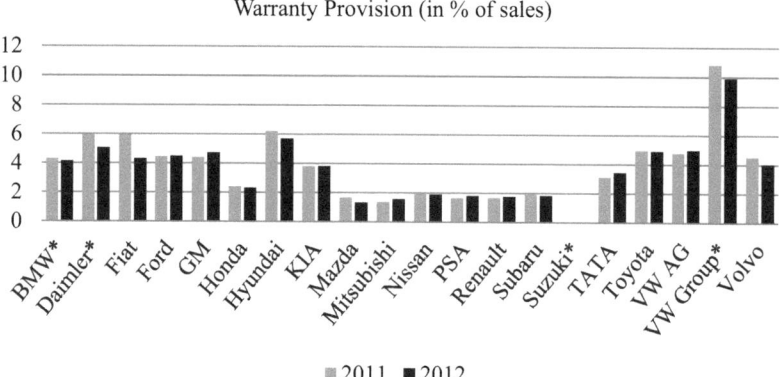

* provision includes also other items

Source: Based on data of annual reports by car manufacturers

Chart 2: Warranty provisions of OEMs in percent of sales

5.3.2 Comparison of Warranty Provisions per Vehicle Sold

The annual reports of the car manufacturers were analyzed in regards to their warranty provision per vehicle sold.

Chart 3 shows that the trend of the warranty provision per unit does not necessarily correlate to the warranty provision in % of sales. The most significant example is provided by Toyota where the warranty provision per unit sold shows a decrease but the warranty provision in % of sales remains on an equal level[336] compared to the previous year. The reason is that the warranty provision shows an increase by 8.5 % but the number of units sold increased by 20.7 %. The revenue increased by 9 %.[337]

---

[333] See tables 5.1 and 5.2 which show the reporting standard used
[334] Volkswagen Group
[335] Volkswagen AG
[336] 4,91 % in 2012 to 4,94 % in 2011
[337] Compares EURO value with exchange rate on the last days of the fiscal year

It has to be considered that some companies have a more diverse product portfolio which influences the total figure in either one or the other direction. For example, Daimler is a manufacturer of premium cars and trucks, and Honda produces 2.8 times[338] more motorcycles than cars. The warranty provisions in the annual reports are not divided by product. This fact could already provide an explanation why Daimler[339] shows the highest value per unit sold and Honda shows a very low amount per unit sold. TATA also has a product range from the low price Nano[340] to heavy trucks and places its warranty provision in between the higher values and the low values. TATA shows an increase in 2012. The explanation in the annual report is that this increase is mainly caused by the volume increase of Jaguar and Land Rover brands.[341] Another reason for the increase could be that TATA provides a 4 year guarantee for heavy trucks starting from January 2013[342]. Also visible in this key figure is the long guarantee period[343] Hyundai gives, which could possibly influence the provision for warranty.

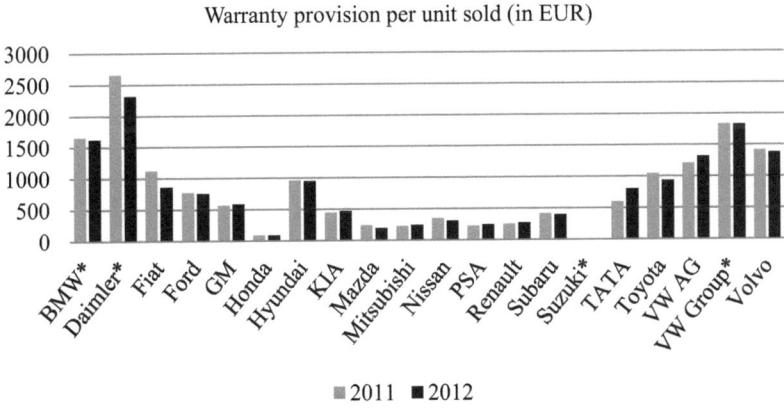

Warranty provision per unit sold (in EUR)

■2011 ■2012

Source: Based on data of annual reports by car manufacturers

* provision includes also other items

Chart 3: Warranty provisions of OEMs per unit sold

---

[338] Cp. Honda (2013), pp. 14, 18.
[339] Cp. Daimler (2012), p. 3 Cover. Daimler provision also includes other items.
[340] Cp. TATA (2013), p. 17.
[341] Cp. TATA (2013), p. 76.
[342] Cp. TATA (2013), p. 54.
[343] See chart 1

5.3.3 Comparison between IFRS and HGB on the Example of Volkswagen

In order to answer the question if the reporting standard has a direct influence on the warranty provision it is necessary to compare the report of the same company which is available in two different standards. Volkswagen reports according to IFRS and HGB. HGB provides an explicit figure for the warranty provision. The report according to IFRS does provide a figure for a provision, which includes primarily warranty claims but also provisions for discounts and bonuses[344]. The share of the warranty claims on the total provision is not available. This is the reason it is not possible to answer the question with the available information. However, it is visible that the difference between the figures provided varies. Warranty in percent of sales according to IFRS is 99 % higher than HGB[345] but the provision compared to the units sold shows that IFRS is only 39 % higher[346]. That could be an indicator, that the figure of warranty provisions compared to the number of vehicles sold is more accurate than the comparison to the sales volume if an statement about quality of the products shall be made. But this statement is only applicable if cars with a comparable price level are considered. An impact of the quality issue of the DSG gear box[347] of Volkswagen in China is not visible in the trend of the warranty provisions. The provision increased only slightly.

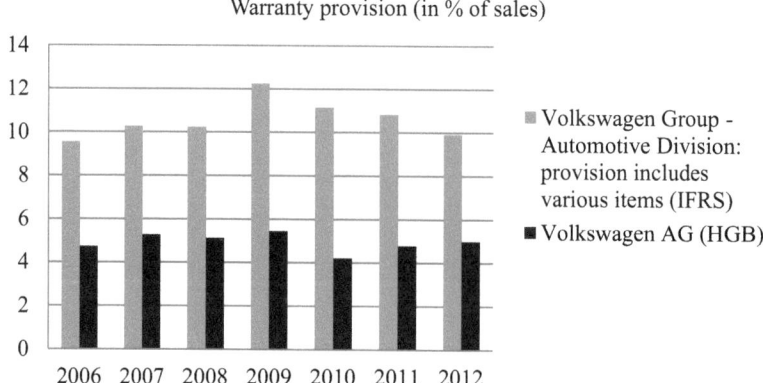

Warranty provision (in % of sales)

Source: Based on data of annual reports by Volkswagen Group and Volkswagen AG

---

[344] Cp. Volkswagen Group (2013), p. 316.
[345] See chart 4. Fiscal year 2012.
[346] See chart 5. Fiscal year 2012.
[347] Cp. chapter 4.3.

Chart 4: Comparison between IFRS and HGB on the example of Volkswagen in percent of sales

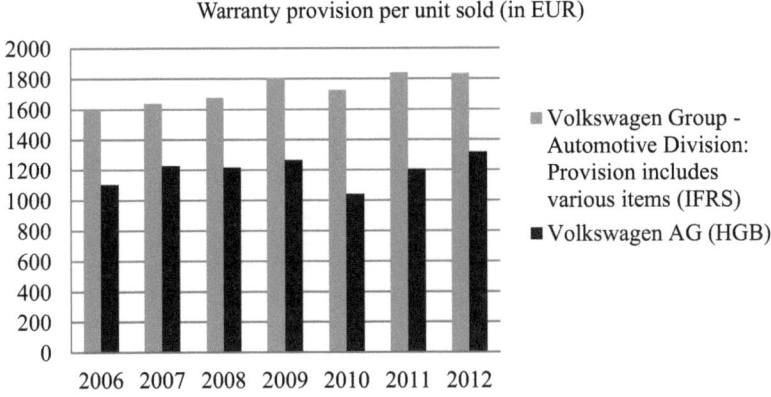

Warranty provision per unit sold (in EUR)

- Volkswagen Group - Automotive Division: Provision includes various items (IFRS)
- Volkswagen AG (HGB)

Source: Based on data of annual reports by Volkswagen Group and Volkswagen AG

Chart 5: Comparison between IFRS and HGB on the example of Volkswagen in EUR per unit sold

5.3.4 Comparison between Toyota and Volkswagen AG from 2006 until 2012

The charts 2 and 3 compare the fiscal years 2011 and 2012 with each other. The two biggest car manufacturers in the world, Toyota and Volkswagen show a similar level of warranty provisions in percentage of sales in 2011 and 2012. But by comparing a longer period, the picture shows a significant difference. Until 2008 Toyota had an outstanding quality reputation.[348] Chart 6 shows that Toyota´s warranty provision in 2009 was only 2.2 % of sales. In 2010 it doubled to 4.4 % due to the floor mat incident.[349] This was an increase of approximately 3.5 billion EUR[350]. At the same time, the warranty provision per vehicle sold increased by approximately 500 EUR. Toyota´s annual report in 2010 announces the establishment of a special committee for quality and notifies the reader in

---

[348] Cp. Liker, J. K. (2004), p. 5.
[349] Cp. Toyota (2011), p. 98.
[350] Exchange rates of the last day of fiscal year.

a whole chapter about the commitment to quality.[351] The cash dividend of Toyota between fiscal year 2008 and fiscal year 2010 dropped by 68 %.[352]

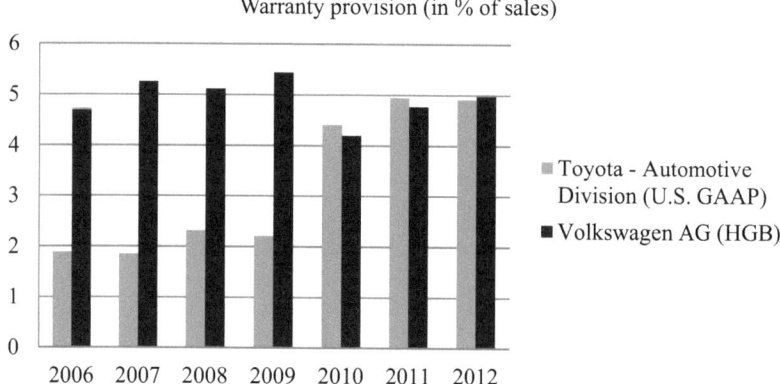

Source: Based on data of annual reports by Toyota and Volkswagen AG 2006 - 2012

Chart 6: Comparison between Toyota and Volkswagen AG in percent of sales

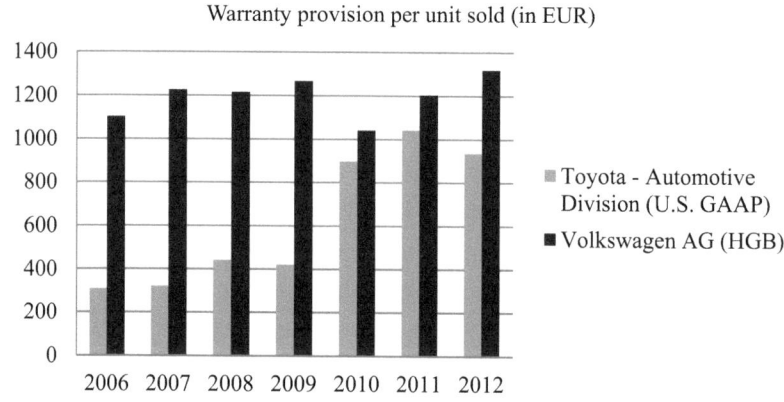

Source: Based on data of annual reports by Toyota and Volkswagen AG 2006 - 2012

Chart 7: Comparison between Toyota and Volkswagen AG in EUR per unit sold

---

[351] Cp. Toyota (2010), pp. 3,4,5.
[352] Cp. Toyota (2010), p. 12.

5.3.5 Comparison between PSA and Renault from 2006 until 2012

The two French car manufacturers PSA and Renault show a decreasing trend in sales over the last years. Between 2006 and 2012 PSA lost 16 % and Renault lost 6 % of revenue. The chart 8 compares the trend of the warranty provisions in percent of sales of these OEMs. Until 2007, PSA had a significant higher value compared to Renault. Since 2008 the values are comparable. PSA shows a 22 % decrease and Renault a 9 % decrease on warranty provisions in percent of sales between 2009 and 2012. PSA explains the reduction of the warranty provision by 71 million EUR in 2012 with the improvement of the vehicle quality.[353] The financial report of Renault mentions warranty as part of the internal Monozukuri[354] program.[355] Chart 9 shows that PSA reduced the warranty provision per unit sold by 33 % to 244 EUR between 2007 and 2012. Renault reduced the warranty provision per unit sold by 22 % to 270 EUR during the same time period. A major difference between the warranty provision in the reports of PSA and Renault is the consideration of third party refunds. Renault deducts supplier reimbursement for warranty cases from the warranty provision[356]. PSA shows the expected refunds from suppliers as an asset in the miscellaneous other receivables.[357]

---

[353] Cp. PSA (2013), p. 85.
[354] Japanese word for a manufacturing improvement philosophy.
[355] Cp. Renault (2013b), p. 10.
[356] Cp. Renault (2013), p. 19.
[357] CP. PSA (2013), p. 84.

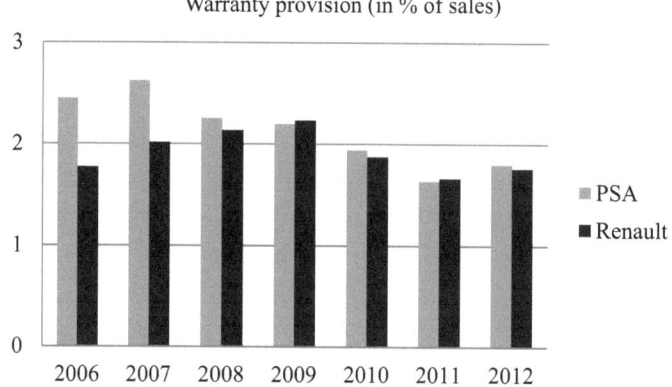

Source: Based on data of annual reports by PSA and Renault 2006 - 2012

Chart 8: Comparison between PSA and Renault in percent of sales

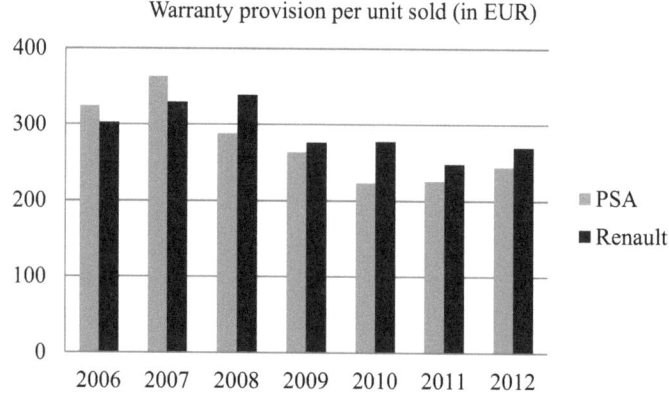

Source: Based on data of annual reports by PSA and Renault 2006 - 2012

Chart 9: Comparison between PSA and Renault in EUR per unit sold

6. Conclusion

Warranty obligations have to be considered a serious risk for car manufacturers due to the high costs related to quality issues which affect high quantities or even result in human injuries due to traffic accidents. With a share of up to 6 % of sales, the amounts accrued for warranty must be considered a major factor in the financial results of a car manufacturing company. These provisions reduce the profit of the business but at the same time also reduce the tax payments. However, statistics of warranties are not published by the international Automobile Organizations.

That marketing tools like a voluntary manufacturer guarantee of up to 5 years or even 7 years are accrued as a provision is the result of the possible room for interpretation the standards and laws give. This is also the case in regards to the presentation of warranty provisions in the annual reports. The international standards desire a harmonization of annual reports but this is not reflected in the used expressions for warranty provisions which are the companies' own creations. The differences in the reporting standards can be considered as a minor impact regarding the amount of warranty provisions. Differences of warranty depending on the market in which the vehicles are sold are mentioned in some of the annual reports but any judgment would require further analysis.

Nevertheless, the documentation in the analyzed annual reports is poor where detail is concerned. Toyota has to be mentioned as a positive example for a transparent report in regards to warranty and quality issues. But it also has to be pointed out that recalls and major warranty issues are only mentioned if they are already part of public knowledge.[358] The German premium manufacturers, BMW and Daimler do not even show an explicit figure for the warranty provision. Volkswagen shows this figure for the Volkswagen AG but not for the complete Volkswagen Group. The reasoning behind this policy would have to be a wild guess. Reputation and prestige is a major marketing factor for these companies. But the investor should have the right to know about the quality performance of his company because the quality strategy is of major importance within the car business. The analysis of the warranty provision helps to understand the situation of the company only if background knowledge is available. But independent from the varying amount, it is also important to note, that the trend is going into the

---

[358] See Toyota floor mat issue

right direction. That means a decrease of warranty related to an improvement in quality. Otherwise the customer satisfaction, which is one of the most important success factors for the car manufacturers, is not probable.

It is also doubtful whether struggling companies due to decreasing market share and decreasing sales, are capable of increasing the quality level by a huge amount within a short time period. Manufacturing companies which need to reduce costs, first slash personnel cost which has the biggest impact.[359] This staff reduction often results in quality issues in production and probably causes an increase in warranty costs than an improvement.

Finally it has to be pointed out that the question, whether the warranty provision is adequate in regards to the amount and is in line with a future oriented quality strategy can only be judged with insider information. That provisions, especially for warranty, can also be used for modeling purposes of the year end results to the desired outcome is common sense. How deep the calculation of warranty provisions is audited cannot be commented within this study but is of major importance for a reliable report.

---

[359] Cp. PSA (2007), p. 9 and PSA (2013b), p. 226. Headcounts of the PSA Automobile division decreased between 2006 and 2012 by 16 %.

Reference list

Alpmann-Pieper, A. (2012): BasisSkript Kaufrecht Werkvertragsrecht, 1st Edition, Alpmann und Schmidt Juristische Lehrgänge Verlagsgesellschaft, Münster 2012

Bertsche, B., Lechner, G. (1999): Zuverlässigkeit im Maschinenbau – Ermittlung von Bauteil- und System-Zuverlässigkeiten, 2nd Edition, Springer Berlin, Heidelberg 1999

Bertsche, B. (2008): Reliability in Automotive and Mechanical Engineering, Springer Berlin, Heidelberg 2008

Buchholz, R. (2013): Grundzüge des Jahresabschlusses nach HGB und IFRS, 8th Edition, Franz Vahlen, Munich 2013

Christ, S. (2011): Vertragsfreiheit in China – Ein Vergleich zwischen chinesischem und deutschem Vertragsrecht, Diplomica Verlag, Hamburg 2011

Dippe, A. (2008): Einsatz von Qualitätstechniken in der Entwicklung komplexer Systeme – Entwicklung eines Vorgehensmodells am Beispiel der Automobilindustrie, Diss., TU Berlin, Shaker, Aachen 2008

Döring, U., Führich, E., Klunzinger, E., Oehlrich, M., Richter, T. (2012): Aktuelle Wirtschaftsgesetze 2013 - Die wichtigsten Wirtschaftsgesetze für Studierende, 5th Edition, Franz Vahlen, Munich 2013

Hertog, Ch., (2008): Die Kosten der Nichtqualität – Qualitätsbezogene Wirtschaftlichkeitsanalyse im Umfeld der Automobilindustrie, VDM Verlag Dr. Müller, Saarbrücken 2008

International Automotive Task Force (2009): Technische Spezifikation ISO/TS16949 Qualitätsmanagementsysteme – Besondere Anforderungen bei Anwendung von ISO 9001:2008 für die Serien- und Ersatzteil-Produktion in der Automobilindustrie, ISO, Genf 2009

Joos, B. (2013): Der Werkvertrag im Recht der VR China, Diss., Verlag Dr. Kovac, Hamburg 2013

Kaiser, S. (2008): Rückstellungsbilanzierung – Ansatz- und Bewertungskonzeptionen für Rückstellungen nach HGB, IFRS und US-GAAP am Beispiel von Stilllegungsverpflichtungen, Gabler Edition Wissenschaft, Wiesbaden 2008

Levine, D. M. (2006): Statistics For Six Sigma Green Belts – with MINITAB and JMP, Pearson-Prentice Hall, Upper Saddle River 2006

Liker, J.K. (2004): The Toyota Way – 14 Management Principles from the World's Greatest Manufacturer, McGraw-Hill, New York 2004

Melcher, W., David, K., Skowronek, T. (2013): Rückstellungen in der Praxis – Anwendungsfälle nach HGB und IFRS, Wiley, Weinheim 2013

NWB Redaktion (2010): Wichtige Steuergesetze mit Durchführungsverordnung, 59th Edition, Status of 1st of January 2010, Verlag Neue Wirtschafts-Briefe, Herne 2010

Prabhakar Murthy, D.N., Blischke, W.R. (2006): Warranty Management and Product Manufacture, Springer Verlag London Limited, London 2006

Precht, M., Kraft, R., Bachmaier, M. (1999): Angewandte Statistik 1 – Beschreibende und Explorative Statistik – Wahrscheinlichkeitsrechnung – Zufallsvariablen und Statistische Maßzahlen – Wichtige Verteilungen – Beurteilende Statistik – Vertrauensintervalle – Hypothesentests , 6th Edition, Oldenburg, Munich 1999

Rehbehn, R., Bülent Yurdukul, Z. (2003): Mit Six Sigma zu Business Excellence – Strategien, Methoden, Praxisbeispiele, Siemens Aktiengesellschaft, Berlin 2003

Rothoeft, D. D. (2004): Rückstellungen nach § 249 HGB und ihre Entsprechungen in den US-GAAP und IAS, Max-Planck-Institut für ausländisches und internationales Privatrecht, Tübingen 2004

Scheffler, E. (2009): Bilanzen richtig lesen – Rechnungslegung nach HGB und IAS/IFRS, 8th Edition, Beck-Wirtschaftsberater, Deutscher Taschenbuchverlag, Munich 2009

Scheffler, E. (2011): IFRS Kennzahlen – Dictionary – IFRS Financial Ratios, C.H. Beck, Munich 2011

Sternstein, M. (1996): Statistics, Barron´s Educational Series, New York 1996

Tamme, A. (1996): Rückrufkosten – Haftung und Versicherung, Diss., Verlag Versicherungswirtschaft, Karlsruhe 1996

VDA - Verband der Automobilindustrie e. V. (2000): Volume 3 - Zuverlässigkeitssicherung bei Automobilherstellern und Lieferanten, part 1 – Zuverlässigkeitsmanagement, 3rd Edition, VDA Qualitätsmanagement-Center, Oberursel 2000

VDA - Verband der Automobilindustrie e. V. (2008): Volume 3 - Zuverlässigkeitssicherung bei Automobilherstellern und Lieferanten, part 2 – Zuverlässigkeits-Methoden und -Hilfsmittel, 3rd Edition, VDA Qualitätsmanagement-Center, Oberursel 2008

VDA - Verband der Automobilindustrie e. V. (2010): Volume 4 - Quality Assurance in the Process Landscape – General, risk analyses, methods, process models – 8D Method, 1st. Edition, VDA Qualitätsmanagement-Center, Oberursel 2010

Wagenhofer, A. (2013): Kodex des Internationalen Rechts – IAS/IFRS Internationale Rechnungslegung 2013/14, 13th Edition, Doralt, W., Linde, Wien 2013

Wawerla, M., (2008): Risikomanagement von Garantieleistungen – Methodische Identifikation, Beurteilung, Steuerung und Überwachung der Risiken von Garantieleistungen im Maschinen- und Anlagenbau, Diss., Universität Karlsruhe, Shaker Verlag, Aachen 2008

Wiewiórowska-Domagalska, A. (2013): Consumer Sales Guarantees in the European Union, Diss., Sellier European Law Publisher, Munich 2013

Williams, M. A. (2008): Six Sigma Pocket Guide – Werkzeuge zur Prozessverbesserung, Rath & Strong Management Consultants, Lexington, MA 2006, TÜV Media GmbH, Köln 2008

Printmedia

Doll, N. (2013): Mängel am laufenden Band, in Die Welt Kompakt (2013/08/13), Axel Springer, Berlin 2013

Fasse, M. (2012): Toyota zahlt Milliarden-Entschädigung, in Handelsblatt Nr. 250, (2012/12/28), p. 8.

Henn, Ch. (2013) Die Leistungen der Marken im Vergleich, in: ADAC Motorwelt No. 11, November 2013, ADAC, Munich 2013, p. 56

Herz, C. (2010): Lebenslänglich für Opel-Käfer, in: Handelsblatt 2010/08/06, p. 22

Piltz, B. (2013): Neue Entwicklung im UN-Kaufrecht, in: NJW-Neue Juristische Wochenschrift 35/2013, Beck , Munich 2013, p. 2567-2572

Schneider, M. C., Murphy, M. (2013): System mit Risiko, in Handelsblatt Nr. 221, Wochenende 15./16./17. November 2013, pp. 1, 8, 9.

Internet Sources

ACEA-European Automobile Manufacturers Association (2013): The Automobile Industry Pocket Guide, Brussels 2013:
http://www.acea.be/images/uploads/files/POCKET_GUIDE_13.pdf , download on 2014/01/03

ADAC-Liste zur Abgrenzung Mangel / Verschleiß (2013/08/30):
www.adac.de/infotestrat/fahrzeugkauf-und-verkauf/gebrauchtfahrzeuge/gebrauchtwagenkauf/liste-mangel-verschleiss/ , download on 2013/11/11

Behringer, S. (2011): Wertansätze für Gewährleistungsrückstellungen – Vergleich nach HGB, IFRS und EStG, in: BBK No. 23, December 2nd 2011, NWB Datenbank 2013,

Verlag Neue Wirtschafts-Briefe, Herne 2013, p. 1133, http://www1.nwb-
daten-
bank.de/nwb9/main.aspx?sid=x5yuiajs&kaufschritt=Default&dokurl=content%2fdms%
2fAufsaetze%2fdata%2f000%2f422%2f000422664_0001_index.xml&shigh=Wertans%
e4tze%2bGew%e4hrleistungsr%fcckstellungen&aktion=DokumentAnzeigen , download on 2013/09/01

Behriger, S. (2012): Gewährleistungsrückstellungen nach HGB, IFRS und EStG, in:
BBK No. 20, October 19th 2012, NWB Datenbank 2013, Verlag Neue Wirtschafts-
Briefe, Herne 2013, p. 945: http://www1.nwb-
daten-
bank.de/nwb9/main.aspx?sid=tmduv0fj&kaufschritt=Default&dokurl=content%2fdms
%2fAufsaetze%2fdata%2f000%2f447%2f000447849_0001_index.xml&shigh=Gew%e
4hrleistungsr%fcckstellungen%2bHGB%2bIFRS%2bEStG&aktion=DokumentAnzeige
n , download on 2013/09/01

Bundesbank (2013): Abzinsungszinssätze gemäß § 253 II HGB
www.bundesbank.de/Redaktion/DE/Downloads/Statistiken/Geld_Und_Kapitalmaerkte/
Zinssaetze_Renditen/abzinsungszinssaetze.pdf?_blob=publicationFile , download on
2013/11/18

Engelberth, M. (2013): Gewährleistung, Garantie & Co. – Ansatz- und Bilanzierungsre-
geln in der Praxis, in: NWB No. 15, April 8th 2013, NWB Datenbank 2013, Verlag
Neue Wirtschafts-Briefe, Herne 2013, p. 1110 , http://www1.nwb-
daten-
bank.de/nwb9/main.aspx?sid=tmduv0fj&kaufschritt=Default&dokurl=content%2fdms
%2fAufsaetze%2fdata%2f000%2f461%2f000461947_0001_index.xml&shigh=Gew%e
4hrleistung%2bGarantie%2bCo.%2bAnsatz%2bBilanzierungsregeln%2bPraxis&aktion
=DokumentAnzeigen , download on 2013/09/01

EU Commission notice 2010/C 138 § 69, p. 26. EUR-Lex – Access to European Union
law, http://eur-
lex.europa.eu/LexUriServ/LexUriServ.do?uri=OJ:C:2010:138:0016:0027:EN:PDF ,
download on 2013/10/31

EU Council Directive 85/374/EEC EUR-Lex – Access to European Union law
http://eur-
lex.europa.eu/LexUriServ/LexUriServ.do?uri=OJ:L:1985:210:0029:0033:EN:PDF ,
download on 2013/10/31

EU DIRECTIVE 1999/44/EC OF THE EUROPEAN PARLIAMENT AND OF THE
COUNCIL (2013) EUR-Lex – Access to European Union law, http://eur-
lex.europa.eu/smartapi/cgi/sga_doc?smartapi!celexplus!prod!CELEXnumdoc&lg=EN&
numdoc=32011L0083 , download on 2013/10/31

Hessisches Ministerium der Finanzen (2011): Haushaltsplan des Landes Hessen für das Jahr 2012, Wiesbaden 2011 http://verwaltung.hessen.de/irj/go/km/docs/Hessen/HMdF/Applikationen/Gesamthausha ltsplaene/Gesamtplan%202012.pdf , download on 2014/01/03

Kraftfahrt - Bundesamt (2013): Jahresbericht 2012, Kraftfahrt - Bundesamt, Flensburg 2013, http://www.kba.de/cln_031/nn_124834/DE/Presse/Jahresberichte/jahresbericht__2012.h tml , download on 2013/10/31

Mercer (2013), Verlauf des Zinssatzen 2010/2011/2012/2013, iBoxx corporate 10+ index: http://www.mercer.de/articles/Rechnungszins, download on 2013/11/25

OANDA (2013), Exchange rates, www.oanda.com

OICA (2012), Motorization rate 2011-worldwide, Paris 2012: http://www.oica.net/wp-content/uploads/2013/09/francfort-2013_carte.pdf , download on 2014/01/03

Regulation (EC) No 1606/2002 OF THE EUROPEAN PARLIAMENT AND OF THE COUNCIL of 19 July 2002 on the application of international accounting standards. EUR-Lex – Access to European Union law, http://eur-lex.europa.eu/LexUriServ/LexUriServ.do?uri=OJ:L:2010:186:0001:0009:EN:PDF , download on 2013/10/31

United Nations (2010): Convention on Contracts for the Internationals Sale of Goods, UNITED NATIONS PUBLICATION Sales No. E. 10.V.14, New York 2010 , http://www.uncitral.org/pdf/english/texts/sales/cisg/V1056997-CISG-e-book.pdf , download on 2013/10/31

Annual Reports

BMW Group (2012): Annual Report 2011, Bayerische Motoren Werke, Munich 2012: http://www.bmwgroup.com/e/0_0_www_bmwgroup_com/investor_relations/corporate_ events/hauptversammlung/2012/BMW-Annual-Report-2011.pdf , download on 2013/10/25

BMW Group (2012): BMW Geschäftsbericht 2011, Bayerische Motoren Werke, Munich 2012: http://geschaeftsbericht2011.bmwgroup.com/bmwgroup/annual/2011/gb/German/pdf/be richt2011.pdf , download on 2013/10/25

BMW Group (2013): Annual Report 2012, Bayerische Motoren Werke, Munich 2013: http://annual-report2012.bmwgroup.com/bmwgroup/annual/2012/gb/English/pdf/report2012.pdf , download on 2013/10/25

BMW Group (2013): Jahresabschluss der BMW AG 2012, Bayerische Motoren Werke, Munich 2013:
http://www.bmwgroup.com/d/0_0_www_bmwgroup_com/investor_relations/finanzberi chte/geschaeftsberichte/2012/_pdf/BMW_AG_Jahresabschluss_2012_de.pdf , download on 2013/10/25

Daimler (2012): Annual Report 2011 – Innovation and Growth, Daimler AG, Stuttgart 2012:
http://www.daimler.com/Projects/c2c/channel/documents/2125319_Daimler_2011_Ann ual_Report.pdf , download on 2013/10/25

Daimler (2013): Annual Report 2012, Daimler AG, Stuttgart 2013:
http://www.daimler.com/Projects/c2c/channel/documents/2287152_Daimler_Annual_R eport_2012.pdf , download on 2013/10/25

Fiat (2012): Annual Report at 31 December 2011 – 106th financial year, Fiat S.p.A., Turin 2012: http://www.fiatspa.com/en-US/investor_relations/financial_reports/FiatDocuments/Bilanci/2011/Fiat_AnnualRepor t_2011_ENG.pdf , download on 2013/10/25

Fiat Group (2013): Annual Report at 31 December 2012, Fiat S.p.A., Turin 2013:

http://www.fiatspa.com/en-US/investor_relations/financial_reports/FiatDocuments/Bilanci/2012/FiatGroup_Annua l_Report_2012_ENG.pdf , download on 2013/10/25

Ford Motor Company (2012): 2011 Annual Report – Go Further, Ford Motor Company, Dearborn 2012: http://corporate.ford.com/doc/2011_annual_report.pdf , download on 2013/10/25

Ford Motor Company (2013): 2012 Annual Report – Profitable Growth for All, Ford Motor Company, Dearborn 2013: http://corporate.ford.com/doc/ar2012-2012%20Annual%20Report.pdf , download on 2013/10/25

General Motors Company (2012): 2011 Annual Report – Vision in Motion, General Motors Company, Detroit 2012:
http://www.gm.com/content/dam/gmcom/COMPANY/Investors/Stockholder_Informati on/PDFs/2011_GM_Annual_Report.pdf , download on 2013/10/25

General Motors Company (2013): 2012 Annual Report, General Motors Company, Detroit 2013:
http://www.gm.com/content/dam/gmcom/COMPANY/Investors/Stockholder_Informati on/PDFs/2012_GM_Annual_Report.pdf , download on 2013/10/25

Honda (2012): Annual Report 2012, Honda Motor Co., Ltd., Tokyo 2012:
http://world.honda.com/investors/library/annual_report/2012/honda2012ar-all-e.pdf , download on 2013/10/25

Honda (2013): Annual Report 2013, Honda Motor Co., Ltd., Tokyo 2013: http://world.honda.com/investors/library/annual_report/2013/honda2013ar-all-e.pdf , download on 2013/10/25

Hyundai Motor Company (2012): 2011 Hyundai Annual Report, Hyundai Motor Company, Seoul 2013: http://worldwide.hyundai.com/WW/Corporate/InvestorRelations/FinancialInformation/ FinancialStatements/index.html , download on 2013/10/25

Hyundai Motor Company (2013): 2012 Hyundai Annual Report, Hyundai Motor Company, Seoul 2013: http://worldwide.hyundai.com/WW/Corporate/InvestorRelations/FinancialInformation/ FinancialStatements/index.html , download on 2013/10/25

KIA Motors (2012): Annual Report 2011, KIA Motors, Seoul 2012: http://www.kmcir.com/eng/library/annual.asp , download on 2013/10/25

KIA Motors (2013): Annual Report 2012, KIA Motors, Seoul 2013: http://www.kmcir.com/eng/library/annual.asp , download on 2013/10/25

Mazda (2012): Annual Report 2012, Mazda Motor Corporation, Hiroshima 2012: http://www.mazda.com/investors/library/annual/2012/zip/MazdaAr12_e.zip , download on 2013/10/25

Mazda (2013): Annual Report 2013, Mazda Motor Corporation, Hiroshima 2013: http://www.mazda.com/investors/library/annual/2013/pdf/MazdaAr13_e.pdf , download on 2013/10/25

Mitsubishi Corporation (2012): Financial Section of Annual Report 2012, Mitsubishi Corporation, Tokyo 2012: http://www.mitsubishicorp.com/jp/en/ir/library/ar/pdf/financial/2012/all.pdf , download on 2013/10/25

Mitsubishi Corporation (2013): Annual Report 2013 –, Mitsubishi Corporation, Realizing our vision for 2020, Tokyo 2013: http://www.mitsubishicorp.com/jp/en/ir/library/ar/pdf/areport/2013/all.pdf , download on 2013/10/25

Mitsubishi Corporation (2013): Financial Section of Annual Report 2013, Mitsubishi Corporation, Tokyo 2013: http://www.mitsubishicorp.com/jp/en/ir/library/ar/pdf/financial/2013/all.pdf , download on 2013/10/25

Mitsubishi Motors Corporation (2013): Annual Report 2013, Harnessing Emerging Market Dynamism, Mitsubishi Motors, Tokyo 2013: http://www.mitsubishi-motors.com/content/dam/com/ir_en/pdf/anual/2013/annual2013_2.pdf , download on 2013/10/25

Mitsubishi Motors Corporation (2013): Financial results 2013, Mitsubishi Motors, Tokyo 2013: http://www.mitsubishi-motors.com/content/dam/com/ir_en/pdf/financial/2013/131029-2b.pdf , download on 2013/10/25

Nissan Motor Company (2012): Fiscal year 2011 financial results, Nissan Motor Co., Ltd., Yokohama 2012: http://www.nissan-glob-al.com/EN/DOCUMENT/PDF/FINANCIAL/ABSTRACT/2011/2011results_financialresult_521_e.pdf , download on 2013/10/25

Nissan Motor Company (2013): Fiscal year 2012 financial results, Nissan Motor Co., Ltd., Yokohama 2013: http://www.nissan-glob-al.com/EN/DOCUMENT/PDF/FINANCIAL/PRESEN/2012/2012results_presentation_825_e.pdf , download on 2013/10/25

Nissan Motor Company (2013): Annual Report 2013, Nissan Motor Co., Ltd., Yokohama 2013: http://www.nissan-global.com/EN/DOCUMENT/PDF/AR/2012/AR2012_E_All.pdf , download on 2013/10/25

PSA Peugeot Citroën (2012): 2006 Annual Results, Peugeot S.A., Paris 2007: http://www.psa-peugeot-citroen.com/en/financial-results , download on 2013/10/25

PSA Peugeot Citroën (2012): 2007 Annual Results, Peugeot S.A., Paris 2008: http://www.psa-peugeot-citroen.com/en/financial-results , download on 2013/10/25

PSA Peugeot Citroën (2012): 2008 Annual Results, Peugeot S.A., Paris 2009: http://www.psa-peugeot-citroen.com/en/financial-results , download on 2013/10/25

PSA Peugeot Citroën (2012): 2009 Annual Results, Peugeot S.A., Paris 2010: http://www.psa-peugeot-citroen.com/en/financial-results , download on 2013/10/25

PSA Peugeot Citroën (2012): 2010 Annual Results, Peugeot S.A., Paris 2011: http://www.psa-peugeot-citroen.com/en/financial-results , download on 2013/10/25

PSA Peugeot Citroën (2012): 2011 Annual Results, Peugeot S.A., Paris 2012: http://www.psa-peugeot-citroen.com/en/financial-results , download on 2013/10/25

PSA Peugeot Citroën (2013): 2012 Annual Results, Peugeot S.A., Paris 2013: http://www.psa-peugeot-citroen.com/en/financial-results , download on 2013/10/25

PSA Peugeot Citroën (2013): 2012 Registration Document, Peugeot S.A., Paris 2013: http://www.psa-peugeot-citroen.com/en/financial-publications/253 , download on 2014/01/03

Renault Group (2007): Annual Report 2006, Renault S.A., Boulougne-Billancourt 2007: http://www.renault.com/en/Finance/presentations-et-documents/Pages/documents-et-presentations.aspx , download on 2013/10/25

Renault Group (2008): Annual Report 2007, Renault S.A., Boulougne-Billancourt 2008: http://www.renault.com/en/Finance/presentations-et-documents/Pages/documents-et-presentations.aspx , download on 2013/10/25

Renault Group (2009): Annual Report 2008, Renault S.A., Boulougne-Billancourt 2009: http://www.renault.com/en/Finance/presentations-et-documents/Pages/documents-et-presentations.aspx , download on 2013/10/25

Renault Group (2009): 2008 Consolidated Financial Statements, Renault S.A., Boulougne-Billancourt 2009: http://www.renault.com/en/Finance/presentations-et-documents/Pages/documents-et-presentations.aspx , download on 2013/10/25

Renault Group (2010): Annual Report 2009, Renault S.A., Boulougne-Billancourt 2010: http://www.renault.com/en/Finance/presentations-et-documents/Pages/documents-et-presentations.aspx , download on 2013/10/25

Renault Group (2010): 2009 Consolidated Statements, Renault S.A., Boulougne-Billancourt 2010: http://www.renault.com/en/Finance/presentations-et-documents/Pages/documents-et-presentations.aspx , download on 2013/10/25

Renault Group (2011): Annual Report 2010, Renault S.A., Boulougne-Billancourt 2011: http://www.renault.com/en/Finance/presentations-et-documents/Pages/documents-et-presentations.aspx , download on 2013/10/25

Renault Group (2012): An ambitious strategy, for a brand in full renewal 2011 Annual Report, Renault S.A., Boulougne-Billancourt 2012: http://www.renault.com/en/Finance/presentations-et-documents/Pages/documents-et-presentations.aspx , download on 2013/10/25

Renault Group (2012): 2011 Financial Results, Renault S.A., Boulougne-Billancourt 2012: http://www.renault.com/en/Finance/presentations-et-documents/Pages/documents-et-presentations.aspx , download on 2013/10/25

Renault Group (2013): A World of Mobility 2012 Annual Report, Renault S.A., Boulougne-Billancourt 2013: http://www.renault.com/en/Finance/presentations-et-documents/Pages/documents-et-presentations.aspx , download on 2013/10/25

Renault Group (2013): 2012 Financial Results, Renault S.A., Boulougne-Billancourt 2013: http://www.renault.com/en/Finance/presentations-et-documents/Pages/documents-et-presentations.aspx , download on 2013/10/25

Renault Group (2013): Consolidated financial statements 2012, Renault S.A., Boulougne-Billancourt 2013: http://www.renault.com/en/Finance/presentations-et-documents/Pages/documents-et-presentations.aspx , download on 2013/10/25

Subaru (2013): Annual Report 2013, Fuji Heavy Industries, Tokyo 2013: http://www.fhi.co.jp/english/ir/report/pdf/ar/ar_2013e.pdf , download on 2013/10/25

Suzuki Motor Corporation (2012): Annual Report 2012, Suzuki Motor Corporation, Hamamatsu City 2012: http://www.globalsuzuki.com/ir/library/annualreport/pdf/2012/2012all.pdf , download on 2013/10/25

Suzuki Motor Corporation (2013): Annual Report 2013, Suzuki Motor Corporation, Hamamatsu City 2013: http://www.globalsuzuki.com/ir/library/annualreport/pdf/2013/2013all.pdf , download on 2013/10/25

TATA Motors (2012): TATA Motors 67th Annual Report 2011-2012, TATA Motors Limited, Mumbai 2012: http://tatamotors.com/investors/financials/67-ar-html/pdf/Tata_Motors_AR_2011-12.pdf , download on 2013/10/25

TATA Motors (2013): TATA Motors 68th Annual Report 2012-13, TATA Motors Limited, Mumbai 2013: http://www.tatamotors.com/investors/annualreports-pdf/Annual-Report-2012-2013.pdf , download on 2013/10/25

Toyota Motor Corporation (2006): Annual Report 2006 – Geared toward Continuing Growth, Toyota Motor Corporation, Tokyo 2006: http://www.toyota-global.com/investors/ir_library/annual/pdf/2006/pdf/ar06_e.pdf , download on 2013/10/25

Toyota Motor Corporation (2007): Annual Report 2007 – Building a Platform for Growth, Toyota Motor Corporation, Tokyo 2007: http://www.toyota-global.com/investors/ir_library/annual/pdf/2007/pdf/ar07_e.pdf , download on 2013/10/25

Toyota Motor Corporation (2008): Annual Report 2008 – Driving to Innovate New Value, Toyota Motor Corporation, Tokyo 2008: http://www.toyota-global.com/investors/ir_library/annual/pdf/2008/pdf/ar08_e.pdf , download on 2013/10/25

Toyota Motor Corporation (2009): Annual Report 2009 – The Right Way Forward, Toyota Motor Corporation, Tokyo 2009: http://www.toyota-global.com/investors/ir_library/annual/pdf/2009/pdf/ar09_e.pdf , download on 2013/10/25

Toyota Motor Corporation (2010): Annual Report 2010 – Purpose, Perspective and Passion, Toyota Motor Corporation, Tokyo 2010: http://www.toyota-global.com/investors/ir_library/annual/pdf/2010/pdf/ar10_e.pdf , download on 2013/10/25

Toyota Motor Corporation (2011): Annual Report 2011 – Rewarded with a smile by exceeding your expectations, Toyota Motor Corporation, Tokyo 2011: http://www.toyota-global.com/investors/ir_library/annual/pdf/2011/ar11_e.pdf, download on 2013/10/25

Toyota Motor Corporation (2012): Annual Report 2012 – Our aim: Ever-better cars, Toyota Motor Corporation, Tokyo 2012: http://www.toyota-global.com/investors/ir_library/annual/pdf/2012/ar12_e.pdf, download on 2013/10/25

Toyota Motor Corporation (2013): Annual Report 2013 – True Competitiveness for Sustainable Growth, Toyota Motor Corporation, Tokyo 2013: http://www.toyota-global.com/investors/ir_library/annual/pdf/2013/ar13_e.pdf, download on 2013/10/25

Volkswagen Aktiengesellschaft (2007): Annual Report 2006, Volkswagen AG, Wolfsburg 2007: http://www.volkswagenag.com/content/gb2006/content/en/homepage.bin.html/downloadfilelist/downloadfile/downloadfile/file/Annual_Report_2006.pdf, download on 2013/10/25

Volkswagen Aktiengesellschaft (2008): Driving Ideas., Annual Report 2007, Volkswagen AG, Wolfsburg 2008: http://www.volkswagenag.com/content/vwcorp/info_center/en/publications/2008/03/Annual_Report_2007.bin.html/binarystorageitem/file/VW_AG_GB_2007_en.pdf, download on 2013/10/25

Volkswagen Aktiengesellschaft (2009): Driving Ideas., Annual Report 2008, Volkswagen AG, Wolfsburg 2009: http://www.volkswagenag.com/content/vwcorp/info_center/en/publications/2009/03/GB_2008.bin.html/binarystorageitem/file/Y_2008_e.pdf, download on 2013/10/25

Volkswagen Aktiengesellschaft (2010): Driving Ideas., Annual Report 2009, Volkswagen AG, Wolfsburg 2010: http://www.volkswagenag.com/content/vwcorp/info_center/en/publications/2010/03/Annual_Report_2009.bin.html/binarystorageitem/file/Y_2009_e.pdf, download on 2013/10/25

Volkswagen Aktiengesellschaft (2011): Experience D(r)iversity., Annual Report 2010, Volkswagen AG, Wolfsburg 2011: http://www.volkswagenag.com/content/vwcorp/info_center/en/publications/2011/03/Volkswagen_AG_Geschaeftsbericht_2010.bin.html/binarystorageitem/file/GB_2010_e.pdf, download on 2013/10/25

Volkswagen Aktiengesellschaft (2012): Abschluss Volkswagen AG – Bilanz der Volkswagen AG zum 31. Dezember 2011, Volkswagen AG, Wolfsburg 2012: http://geschaeftsbericht2011.volkswagenag.com/serviceseiten/downloads/files/gesamt_vw_gb11.pdf, download on 2013/10/25

Volkswagen Aktiengesellschaft (2012): Experience D(r)iversity. Vielfalt Erfahren. Sit mnohotvárnost. Annual Report 2011, Volkswagen AG, Wolfsburg 2012: http://annualreport2011.volkswagenag.com/servicepages/downloads/files/entire_vw_ar 11.pdf , download on 2013/10/25

Volkswagen Aktiengesellschaft (2013): Abschluss Volkswagen AG – Bilanz der Volkswagen AG zum 31. Dezember 2012, Volkswagen AG, Wolfsburg 2013: http://www.volkswagenag.com/content/vwcorp/info_center/de/publications/2013/03/Y_ 2012_d.bin.html/binarystorageitem/file/GB+2012_d.pdf , download on 2013/10/25

Volkswagen Aktiengesellschaft (2013): Experience D(r)iversity. Annual Report 2012, Volkswagen AG, Wolfsburg 2013: http://www.volkswagenag.com/content/vwcorp/info_center/en/publications/2013/03/Y_ 2012_e.bin.html/binarystorageitem/file/GB+2012_e.pdf , download on 2013/10/25

Volvo - Geely Sweden AB (2013): Annual Report 2012, Geely Sweden AB, Göteborg 2013: http://www.volvocars.com/SiteCollectionDocuments/TopNavigation/Corporate/Financi als/Annual-Report-2012.pdf , download on 2013/10/25